Ethics and the Early Childhood Educator: Using the NAEYC Code

Third Edition

Stephanie Feeney and Nancy K. Freeman

National Association for the Education of Young Children
Washington, DC

National Association for the Education of Young Children
1313 L Street NW, Suite 500
Washington, DC 20005-4101
202-232-8777 • 800-424-2460
NAEYC.org

NAEYC Books

Senior Director, Content Strategy and Development
Susan Friedman

Editor-in-Chief
Kathy Charner

Senior Creative Design Manager
Audra Meckstroth

Senior Editor
Holly Bohart

Publishing Manager
Francine Markowitz

Creative Designers
Malini Dominey and *Jody West*

Associate Editor
Rossella Procopio

Through its publications program, the National Association for the Education of Young Children (NAEYC) provides a forum for discussion of major issues and ideas in the early childhood field, with the hope of provoking thought and promoting professional growth. The views expressed or implied in this book are not necessarily those of the Association.

Photo credits

Copyright © Erin Donn: vi
Copyright © Julia Luckenbill: xii and 10
Copyright © Syretha Storey: 30
Copyright © Vera Wiest: 16 and 116
Copyright © Getty Images: 50, 80, and 100

Library of Congress Control Number: 2017960253

ISBN: 978-1-938113-33-8

Item 1134

Contents

Foreword

In 2015, after two years of deliberations, the National Academies Press released a seminal report from the Institute of Medicine and the National Research Council— *Transforming the Workforce for Children Birth Through Age 8: A Unifying Foundation.* This important report asserts the decisive neuroscientific evidence about this essential time in a child's life. Because the evidence is clear, the report demands a focus on ensuring that early childhood educators are equipped with the requisite knowledge, skills, and competencies required to teach young children in dynamic, high-quality early learning environments.

Concurrently, NAEYC emerged with a new strategic direction that has energized and prioritized the efforts of early childhood educators. One of the goals of this strategic direction is that NAEYC works to ensure that the early childhood education profession exemplifies excellence and is recognized as vital and performing a critical role in society. NAEYC's desired results include these:

- Professional preparation and development for educators of children from birth through age 8 is aligned with and grounded in NAEYC's standards and delivered in innovative ways.

- Skills, knowledge, competencies, and qualifications are agreed upon by the field and used to define the early care and education profession.

- Early childhood professionals are diverse, effective educators and leaders working within a compensation and recognition system that supports their excellence.

- Professional development and preparation systems support seamless progression for early care and education professionals to advance their education, professional learning, and careers.

In light of this agenda, NAEYC conducted extensive market research to determine why individuals choose to become early childhood educators and what discourages them from remaining in the field and making early childhood education their career. The results of the research in their entirety can be found at NAEYC.org/our-work /initiatives/profession, but in general, early childhood educators are motivated by their love of children and their passion for ensuring that young children start school ready to be successful. They are in agreement that becoming an effective educator requires academic preparation to acquire the necessary knowledge, skills, and competencies. And they are leaving the field because of low pay, minimal benefits, and lack of opportunity for career progression.

The market research also focused on likely voters, who overwhelmingly believe that academic preparation for educators is important and that the competencies and traits of an early childhood educator have a direct effect on the quality of an early childhood program. They also believe that early childhood educators are undercompensated and would support federal and state efforts to increase wages and compensation.

Together, this information leads us to believe that the time has come to boldly move forward to define and advance the early childhood profession. Defining the profession includes agreeing to a name, scope of practice, and the continuum of knowledge, skills, competencies, and academic preparation required for early childhood educators across all early childhood settings. From there it means proposing a licensing, credentialing, and accreditation system for individuals and institutions that will serve as independent confirmation of those individuals' and institutions' qualifications.

You may be curious about what this has to do with NAEYC's Code of Ethical Conduct. For any profession, a code of ethics is a foundational document. As referenced on page 8, a profession has a code of ethics that assures members of society that the profession will serve the public good. A code is a document that spells out the profession's moral obligations to society and its guidelines for moral behavior.

The NAEYC Code of Ethical Conduct is a core document for our collective ability to define our profession. It sits alongside other foundational documents, including NAEYC's six standards for professional preparation, 10 standards for early learning programs, and position statement on developmentally appropriate practice (DAP). The NAEYC Code of Ethical Conduct was created through a consensus process that included some of the best minds in early childhood education.

For *all* early childhood educators—those attaining their CDA or graduating from post-secondary education, directing early learning programs, teaching students in two- and four-year colleges and universities, or rounding out the end of their careers—understanding our professional obligations to the children, families, colleagues, communities, and societies we serve is paramount to our effectiveness as a field.

More important than understanding a code is living it. That is what this book is about. We can read through the NAEYC Code of Ethical Conduct, nod our heads in agreement, and intellectualize it. But if at that point the Code is put back on a shelf and stays there, we have not fully committed to it, and we are not fulfilling our professional obligations. The authors of *Ethics and the Early Childhood Educator* do an outstanding job of helping us apply the Code. To be able to identify a right course in situations involving ethical dilemmas, we need to study, discuss, and make a commitment to the Core Values, Ideals, and Principles of the NAEYC Code and apply them to our practice each day.

There are also implications for our early childhood systems. We must embed the NAEYC Code into coursework at institutions of higher education, informal professional development seminars, and even our state systems. We have to embrace the Core

Values, Ideals, and Principles to such a degree that they are reflected in all of our interactions with teachers, families, colleagues, community, and society.

Each section of the Code is poignant and powerful. I was particularly motivated by the section on our ethical obligation to the community and society. The authors point out our moral obligations to a broader agenda, one that goes beyond an individual child, family, program, community, or state. One that really points to advocacy on behalf of *all* children and families and *all* early childhood educators.

In that vein, I urge you to join NAEYC in advancing a national policy and advocacy agenda. To ensure that all young children have equitable access to developmentally appropriate, high-quality early learning and to advance the early childhood profession, it is essential that early childhood educators link arms and dedicate their time and energy to the policy and advocacy necessary to move a national agenda forward on behalf of the young children we serve and the profession we all love.

—Rhian Evans Allvin
Chief Executive Officer, NAEYC
January 2018

Preface

As an early childhood educator, your actions and words impact children, their families, your colleagues, the community, and society. A knowledge of ethics and of the NAEYC Code of Ethical Conduct provides the guidance all early childhood educators need to be caring, competent professionals.

The Code of Ethical Conduct offers a framework for understanding the moral commitments that are part of your professional relationships. It helps you to know and act upon the values and ideals that guide early childhood educators in their work. It can help you understand your ethical responsibilities and provide guidance for addressing ethical dilemmas you face (an *ethical dilemma* is a predicament that involves conflicting responsibilities and requires a choice between two alternatives that can each be justified).

Ethics and the Early Childhood Educator is written for you—an early childhood teacher or administrator who works with, or is learning to work with, young children, families, and staff in early childhood settings. It introduces the NAEYC Code and explains how to use it. This book will help you

- Learn about the core values and ideals that provide the foundation for practice in the early childhood field
- Appreciate early childhood educators' primary commitment to the welfare of children
- Understand your ethical responsibilities
- Learn to use the Code to formulate well-reasoned resolutions to ethical dilemmas
- Become adept at talking about ethical issues and justifying your positions

The first two editions of *Ethics and the Early Childhood Educator* considered ethical practice from the standpoint of the teacher or caregiver who provides direct service to children in an early childhood education program. This third edition has been expanded to include information for program administrators and those learning to become administrators.

Program administrators (Head Start and other early childhood directors, curriculum specialists, elementary school principals, and others with program oversight responsibilities) encounter many of the same ethical issues as teachers and others who work with children, but they also face unique responsibilities and ethical challenges as they engage in administrative activities. In response to these distinctive challenges, NAEYC developed a supplement to be used with the Code to meet administrators' particular needs. The Supplement for Early Childhood Program Administrators, first adopted by the NAEYC Governing Board in 2006, provides guidance to support administrators in their work and is addressed in various sections throughout this book. The supplement appears in its entirety in Appendix C.

Other revisions to the third edition of *Ethics and the Early Childhood Educator* include updated descriptions of ethical situations, new cases and issues, and updated references.

This book contains

- An introduction to the study of morality and ethics
- The history and rationale for the development of the NAEYC Code and its two supplements
- Strategies for identifying and addressing ethical dilemmas
- Specific chapters that address each of the four sections of the Code
- Approaches for promoting awareness and use of the Code
- The NAEYC Code of Ethical Conduct and Statement of Commitment (see Appendix B) and the Supplement for Early Childhood Program Administrators (see Appendix C)

Our many years of experience in the field and studying ethics as it applies to early childhood education have convinced us that it is important for all early childhood educators to make a commitment to ethical behavior. This latest edition is especially timely because NAEYC is leading an initiative to define the early childhood field and raise its professional status. Understanding your ethical obligations as outlined in the NAEYC Code and applying it to real-life situations are essential aspects of your professional practice.

We hope that reflecting on and practicing the ideas in this book will help you recognize the ethical dimensions of your work, support your efforts to shoulder your professional responsibilities, and guide you as you seek to do what is right for young children and their families. We hope it will be a valuable resource for helping you to confidently answer the question "What should an ethical early childhood educator do?"

—Stephanie Feeney and Nancy K. Freeman

1

An Introduction to Ethics

Early childhood educators work with children at a critical stage in their development. Because we can do so much good and also do harm, our actions *must* be dedicated to the best interests of the young children we serve. We (the authors of this book and our colleagues at the National Association for the Education of Young Children—NAEYC) believe that a moral commitment to children is an important foundation for our work.

This chapter addresses the following introductory topics:

- The early childhood educator as a person
- Personal morality and ethics
- The nature of professions
- Professional values and professional ethics

Your role as an early childhood educator is complex, intense, intimate, and essential to children's well-being. You work closely with children, families, and colleagues. You are expected to meet children's basic needs and nurture their physical, social, emotional, and cognitive development and at the same time support their families as children's first and most important teachers. In your complex role, you are likely to face challenging ethical issues like these:

> In this book, the term *teacher* generally refers to the adult responsible for the direct care and education of a group of children in any early childhood setting (including infant and toddler caregivers and family child care providers). The term *practitioner* also includes administrators. The inclusive term *early childhood educator* refers to individuals in these roles as well as college and university faculty and other adult educators.

- A child in your classroom often acts aggressively and sometimes hurts other children. The other children are afraid of this child, and parents are beginning to complain.
- A parent asks you to not let her 4-year-old son nap at school. She goes to work early in the morning and needs her son to be able to fall asleep at night so they can both be on time in the morning.
- A parent asks you to not let her daughter engage in messy play at school. She says that it is too hard to get paint and clay out of her child's hair and clothing.

- In the staff lounge, you hear a coworker make an insulting joke about children and families of a particular ethnic group. Everyone but you laughs.
- Your program requires you to spend most of the school day teaching academic skills to 4-year-olds using whole group, direct instruction and worksheets rather than developmentally appropriate activities.
- A child comes to school with bruises that she says she got from falling down the stairs. She looks fearful when you ask for more information about what happened.
- A boy in your class likes to wear a princess dress in the dramatic play area. His father arrives one day to see his child wearing the dress and playing princess. Upset, he asks you to never again allow his child to dress as a girl.
- You learn that three children, all boys, have recently been suspended from your program because of its policy stating that aggressive behavior will not be tolerated.
- When school starts in the fall, you learn that over the summer a child in your class of 5-year-olds transitioned from identifying as a girl by the name of Margo to identifying as a boy and wanting to be called Max. The parents, however, insist that you continue to treat and refer to their child as a girl.

See the glossary on page 123 for definitions of words that appear in boldface throughout the book.

If you have faced **ethical issues** like these that require you to determine what is right and wrong, that concern rights and responsibilities, and that affect individuals' personal welfare, it would be natural to use your common sense and best judgment to decide what to do. You might consider what would be good for a particular child, fair to the other children, or what you had done in the past. You might also refer to your program's policies or guidelines to guide your decision-making process.

Although personal decision-making skills and program policies are valuable, they are not always enough to guide professional practice. You are likely to encounter situations in which you must make a difficult decision or work with a family or colleague who challenges decisions you have made based on your best judgment. When that happens, you may find that your previous experience has not prepared you for the situation and your program does not address it in its policies. These situations call for agreed-upon standards of behavior based on the history and collective wisdom of members of your profession. The NAEYC Code of Ethical Conduct was written to provide guidance for understanding and navigating difficult ethical issues in early childhood education.

> **?** Have you encountered challenges similar to those described in this chapter? Where did you turn for help? What would you say to a friend or colleague who is facing one of these situations and asks for your advice?

The Early Childhood Educator as a Person

Your personal attributes, values, and morality and ethics reflect who you are. You bring these features to the workplace, and they form the foundation for who you will be as a professional.

Personal Attributes

Personal attributes are an inherent part of you. They include your temperament (inborn ways of responding to situations, such as activity level and attention span) and disposition (tendencies to respond to experiences in certain ways, such as with cooperation and creativity). Reflect on the personal attributes that you bring to the workplace; they have a powerful influence on your relationships with children, families, and colleagues. Some of the most desirable attributes for early childhood educators are kindness, warmth, sensitivity, the ability to nurture others, self-awareness, respect for others, fairness, passion, perseverance, patience, flexibility, creativity, love of learning, energy, positive outlook, and emotional stability (Colker 2008).

Personal Values

Values are qualities or principles that individuals believe to be desirable or worthwhile and that they prize for themselves, others, and the world in which they live (e.g., truth, beauty, honesty, justice, respect for people and the environment). The priorities and goals you set for yourself and for the children in your care reflect your values.

Your family's values have greatly influenced the personal values you hold today, as have your religious background, community and culture, and life experiences. There are countless ways these personal values guide your personal and professional decisions, including what you choose to do with your time, what you read and watch, what you eat, where you live, the kind of work you do, and what you do for fun and relaxation. If you spend some time reflecting, you will be able to identify your personal values and see what a profound influence they have on your life.

How do your personal values influence what you want to accomplish in your work with children and families? Do you emphasize collaboration or individual achievement? Do you think nurturing creativity is worthwhile? Do you think children's social and emotional development is as important as their cognitive development? Do you think that it is more important for children to learn to respect authority or to question authority? Although you may be passionately attached to your values, you might discover that some of your colleagues and the families you serve have different views.

> **?** Identify some personal values that led you to choose to work with young children. How might these be reflected in your work with children and families?

Personal Morality and Ethics

Morality is what people view as good, right, or proper; their beliefs about their obligations; and ideas about how they should behave. Personal morality begins to develop in the early years. You can probably identify the standards of behavior that the adults you looked up to established in your home, place of worship, and neighborhood. Telling the truth, being fair, putting family first, respecting elders, and treating others with respect are some of the earliest lessons that most of us learned. When you immediately know the right way to respond to a situation that involves an issue like truth, fairness, or respecting others, it is because your personal morality is showing you the way. These early lessons about right and wrong have helped to shape the way you address moral issues during adulthood, including those you encounter in the workplace.

Ethics is the study of right and wrong, duty, and obligation. It involves critical reflection on morality and the ability to examine the moral dimensions of relationships. And it involves choosing between competing values. You are facing an ethical issue when you must decide whether it is more important to always be totally honest with others, even if doing so would likely hurt their feelings, or to be somewhat dishonest in order to avoid hurting their feelings. Choosing either total honesty or telling a "white lie" to avoid hurting someone's feelings is not easy; it requires you to reflect on various factors of the particular situation and to make an ethical decision as to how to balance truthfulness with respect for another's feelings.

You can see that both ethics and morality involve the ability to make choices among values and to make decisions about right and wrong. Although these terms are sometimes used interchangeably, in this book we will use the term *morality* to refer to your personal beliefs about right and wrong and the term *ethics* to refer to conscious deliberation about moral choices.

The Teacher as a Moral Person

You play an important role in teaching children about morality. And while it is not the subject of this book, it is important to remember that you are a role model of ethical conduct and moral values in your day-to-day interactions with children, families, your colleagues, and the community. Certainly, if you want children to be caring and compassionate human beings, you need to be an example of these behaviors. You demonstrate moral behavior by being honest, keeping your promises, being fair, respecting each child as an individual, and treating every child and adult with kindness and respect.

> **?** What are some of your strongly held moral beliefs? Reflect on the experiences in your life that led you to develop these views of morality.

What Is a Profession?

To understand professional ethics and how it contributes to your work as an early childhood educator, you need to understand how professions differ from other occupations. Think about the different roles people play in modern society. Some occupations require practitioners to have specialized knowledge to provide a service to society. These occupations are considered to be **professions.** A **professional** is an individual who carries out the work of a profession. A professional must have specialized educational training, competence, and a commitment to the public good. All professionals are responsible for promoting a social value that is essential to people's well-being; for example, those with medical expertise promote the public's health and legal experts promote justice. Because of their specialized training, professionals are viewed as the only individuals who know how to provide their services. They do something that others cannot do.

Professionals differ from other workers not only because of their special expertise but also because they focus on serving the community rather than their individual self-interest. They are committed to providing a needed public service and making a contribution to society as a whole (Cooper 2003; Moran 1996).

Scholars who study professions have identified a number of criteria to determine if an occupation is a profession (Bassett 2005; Cooper 2003; Feeney 2012; Rhode et al. 2016). The list below briefly describes eight of these criteria that are relevant to early childhood education:

1. A profession has a *commitment to serving a significant social value.* It provides a service that is essential to society and has as its primary goal meeting the needs of others. Professions are dedicated to the public interest. Their members are altruistic and service oriented rather than profit oriented.

2. A profession has a *specialized body of knowledge and expertise* that is based on theory and is applied according to the particular needs of each situation.

3. A profession requires practitioners to participate in *prolonged training* based on principles that involve the use of complex judgment for their application (not a precise set of behaviors that apply in all cases).

4. A profession has rigorous *requirements for entry* into training that are controlled by its members. Professionals are trained at accredited institutions and must graduate from an accredited program; some professionals must also pass an examination to receive a license to practice.

5. Members of the profession have agreed on *standards of practice*—recommended procedures for dealing with situations that are regularly encountered in the workplace. A professional must be aware of and guided by the standards of practice, but the decision about how to act will depend on the specifics of the situation.

6. Based on its important function and the specialized knowledge and skill of its practitioners, a profession is recognized as *the only group in the society that can perform its specialized functions.*

7. Because others in the society do not have the technical knowledge required to oversee their work, professions are characterized by *autonomy*—self-governance that results in internal control over standards and the quality of the services provided.

8. A profession has a *code of ethics* that assures members of the society that it will serve the public good. This code spells out the profession's moral obligations to society and includes guidelines for moral behavior.

Early childhood education is an "emerging profession" because it has some of the elements of recognized professions but lacks others (Feeney 2012). Early childhood education is a diverse field. Early childhood educators have differing levels of education, are employed in a wide variety of settings—including public schools, child development centers (large and small, nonprofit and for profit, and public and privately sponsored), and family child care homes—and do many different types of work. While the majority of early childhood educators work directly with young children and families, others are administrators, teach adults who work or will work with young children, or work on behalf of young children in agencies or organizations.

NAEYC is leading an initiative to focus on the professionalization of the field. Power to the Profession is a national collaboration to define the early childhood profession by establishing a unifying framework for career pathways, knowledge and competencies, qualifications, standards, and compensation. For more information about this initiative, go to NAEYC.org.

In spite of this diversity, the field is working to advance its professional status. Progress has been made in recent years on criteria such as specialized knowledge and expertise, training based on agreed-upon principles of best practices, identified competencies for various positions in the field, and standards of practice. The criteria of rigorous requirements for entry into the field, extensive training, and autonomy still present serious challenges. Because early childhood educators serve the important social function of providing care and education for the nation's youngest and most vulnerable citizens, it is significant that the field has a code of professional ethics that its practitioners strive to live by—even as the field moves toward achieving other criteria of professionalization.

Professional Values and Professional Ethics

Because the public puts its trust in professionals to serve the common good, professionals are expected to commit themselves to behaving ethically. Although each person's values and morality are important, they are not enough to guide professional behavior. Not everyone adopts the same values or learns the same moral lessons; those who share the same beliefs may not apply them in the same way, and workplace issues may not be addressed by the morality they grew up with.

As an early childhood educator, you will find that morality based on your personal values may not provide the guidance you need when a mother asks you to be certain her child doesn't nap, even when he needs the rest; when a colleague makes an insulting joke about an ethnic group; when a program expects you to teach 4-year-olds academic skills using worksheets; or when faced with any of the other dilemmas described at the beginning of this chapter. These situations all have a moral dimension and challenge teachers to discern and do the right thing.

Personal attributes, values, and morality need to be complemented with professional values and standards of ethical behavior if all early childhood educators are going to behave in consistent ways and speak with one voice about their commitments to young children and their families.

Professional Core Values

Professional core values are commitments that are consciously and knowingly embraced by the members of a profession because they contribute to society. These values are different from an individual's personal values. They are not a matter of preference; they are values that the members of the profession have agreed are essential to their work. These values grow from the history, knowledge base, and traditions of the profession and help shape its aspirations and beliefs about desirable practice. Professional core values provide the foundation for discussions of professional ethics and the development of moral guidelines as expressed in a code of ethics.

Professionals who deal directly with the welfare of people have a special obligation to behave in ways that nurture and benefit those they serve. Essential core values for professions that are based on human relationships, such as early childhood education, include caring, compassion, empathy, respect for others, and trustworthiness.

> **?** With a colleague or classmate, brainstorm a list of commitments to children, families, colleagues, and community and society that you think all early childhood educators should hold. Compare your list to the list of Core Values in the NAEYC Code of Ethical Conduct. (See page 128 in Appendix B.) How are the two similar or different? Reflect on some possible reasons for differences.

Professional Ethics and Codes of Professional Ethics

Professional ethics are the moral commitments of a profession that extend and enhance the personal morality practitioners bring to their work. Professional ethics concern actions of right and wrong in the workplace and help individuals resolve moral dilemmas. Professionals engage in critical reflection that informs the development of the profession's code of ethics.

A **code of ethics** is a document that expresses the field's commitment to live up to society's expectations (Schwimmer & Maxwell 2017). By expressing a profession's sense of mission, defining its core values, and providing guidance for addressing conflicting responsibilities in the workplace, a code of ethics helps to instill confidence that its members deserve the public's trust. A profession's code of ethics also helps its members see that they are part of a community, shifting their thinking from "me" to "we."

A code of ethics provides the following for a profession:

- A vision of what professionals should be like and how they should behave
- A statement of commonalities shared by everyone in the field regardless of the setting they work in or the training they have received
- An introduction to the moral commitments of the profession for those entering it
- Guidance in making choices that best promote the interests of those served
- A tool for recognizing and articulating core values
- Guidance for understanding and prioritizing responsibilities in order to find wise resolutions to ethical dilemmas
- Support for a professional who takes a courageous, risky stand
- A justification for a difficult decision
- A resource for generating discussion
- Information for the broader community about the profession's values and views of acceptable professional behavior
- Assurance to members of the society that professional practitioners will behave in accordance with moral standards (Feeney 2012; Maxwell & Schwimmer 2016; Schwimmer & Maxwell 2017; Stonehouse 1998)

Codes of ethics vary among professions. While some are general and aspirational, others provide specific guidance by spelling out members' ethical responsibilities and offering guidelines for resolving the recurring dilemmas that occur in their daily work (Schwimmer & Maxwell 2017).

Professional codes of ethics are grounded in **moral philosophy**—the branch of philosophy concerned with the systematic study of morality, including explorations of what it means to do right or wrong, good or evil. Chapter 3 briefly explores some approaches to moral philosophy that may be helpful as you reflect on possible resolutions to the ethical dilemmas you face in your work (see "Applying Theories of Moral Philosophy" on page 26).

What About Laws and Regulations?

A profession's code of ethics is not the same thing as the policies, regulations, and legal obligations that govern the workplace. An important difference is that a code of ethics addresses individual *moral* responsibilities, not legal requirements. Not every aspect of professional morality is likely to be addressed by laws, and some laws may not have moral content or may even be determined to be immoral.

In addition, while laws are enforced by penalties imposed by civic authorities like local police departments, personal morality is enforced by an individual's conscience. You may feel guilty or ashamed if you do something that violates your personal morality, but if you have not broken any laws there is no penalty for your actions. Professional morality, as expressed in a code of ethics, may be enforced by sanctions decided on by professional peers rather than an outside authority.

Codes of ethics also differ from regulations, such as those that govern the operation of early childhood programs. Regulations apply to organizations, whereas codes provide guidance for individuals. In addition, members of the profession create their codes of ethics, while the laws, policies, and regulations that govern the profession are frequently written by individuals who are not part of that field (Schwimmer & Maxwell 2017).

Although regulations and laws are important because they provide basic protections for clients, and they may overlap with a code of ethics in some ways, the profession's code represents a higher standard. A code describes the ideals of the profession and the obligations of individual practitioners.

———————

Fortunately, early childhood education doesn't leave its practitioners to puzzle out how to behave ethically on their own. The NAEYC Code of Ethical Conduct provides a shared common ground for those who strive to honor their ethical obligations and to do the right thing in the workplace. The field's core values lay the foundation for the Ideals and Principles set forth in the Code. These ethical guidelines help you to weigh and balance conflicting responsibilities and find resolutions to the dilemmas you are likely to encounter in your work (Freeman & Feeney 2016).

Ethical Issues and Best Practices

Best practices regarding what and how to teach children are based on teachers' knowledge of child development; each child's individual strengths, interests, and needs; the social and cultural context within which each child lives; and research-based approaches to curriculum. This knowledge guides teachers' decision making both as they plan for each child and the group and as they make in-the-moment decisions during their interactions with children. Early childhood educators need to know current views about best practices and understand the difference between ethical behavior and best practices.

2

The NAEYC Code of Ethical Conduct

More than 40 years ago, NAEYC led an effort to develop a code of ethics that would address the ethical dimensions of working with young children. This chapter describes

- Why the Code was created
- How it is organized
- How the Code has, since it was first published, responded to changes in society and in the field of early childhood education

Why Does Early Childhood Education Need a Code of Ethics?

In NAEYC's first book about ethics, *Ethical Behavior in Early Childhood Education* ([1978] 1991), authors Lilian Katz and Evangeline Ward described some of the reasons early childhood educators need a code of ethics and discussed why it is so important for those who teach and care for young children to be aware of the ethical dimensions of their work. This work provided an important impetus for the development of the NAEYC Code of Ethical Conduct.

Despite the many changes that have occurred in the field of early childhood education since that time, two of the reasons that helped Katz and Ward identify the need for a code of ethics are still very relevant today.

Young Children Are Vulnerable

The most compelling reason for having and using a code of ethics for the early childhood field is that educators are responsible for children who are vulnerable and often powerless.

Adults are larger and stronger and control resources that children need, so they must act in ways that support rather than jeopardize children's welfare. For example, some of the cases outlined in Chapters 6 and 7 describe situations in which a colleague's or administrator's actions—or lack of action—could endanger children.

Young children cannot defend themselves when teachers are uncaring, thoughtless, or abusive. Infants and toddlers are not able to communicate in words. Even when an older child is able to describe harmful or neglectful behavior, the family may not know that what occurred was inappropriate, may not understand the impact of that mistreatment on their child, and may not be able to ensure that their child will not be treated inappropriately again.

What's more, some individuals who work with young children have not been trained in early childhood education. Their lack of specialized knowledge and competence may increase the likelihood that they will behave unprofessionally. For example, they might show a preference for children who are particularly bright or attractive or react in demanding and punitive ways to children who are active and boisterous. In addition, they may not be confident in their understanding of how to work effectively with young children, which may increase the likelihood that they will be easily influenced when a family member or colleague suggests they do something that is not in children's best interests. In Chapter 5, you will read about situations in which studying the Code helps teachers consider the benefits of certain routines and activities for children's development and weigh these against families' requests to not allow their children to participate in them.

Having a code of ethics helps you understand your ethical obligations, resist using inappropriate practices, and approach ethical issues wisely.

The NAEYC Code of Ethical Conduct (shown here in brochure form) is based on the core values of the early childhood field. It provides guidelines for professional conduct and addressing ethical issues. The Code is designed to protect young children by helping their educators identify actions that are right, just, and fair.

Multiplicity of Clients

Another reason a code of ethics is important is that early childhood educators serve children, families, colleagues (both coworkers and employers), and the community, and sometimes these parties have competing interests. For example, in the Messy Play case in Chapter 5, the teacher must balance her conflicting responsibilities to a child and the child's mother when the mother requests that her child not be permitted to engage in messy play because of the challenges involved in cleaning her child's clothes and hair. Many early childhood educators would feel that their primary responsibility and allegiance is to the child and that the child would likely benefit from hands-on sensory experiences. But when a parent requests that her own needs take priority, it can be hard to decide the best course of action. Under some circumstances, you might believe that the needs of the parent should come first.

Early childhood program administrators also serve multiple clients. In addition to children, families, and the community, administrators have responsibilities to the individuals who work in their program or school as well as their boards of directors, sponsoring agencies, and funders.

When you encounter situations with multiple **stakeholders,** a code of ethics can help you decide how to prioritize your responsibilities. Stakeholders are individuals involved in or affected by a course of action and include children, families, employees, administrators, and the community.

History and Organization of the NAEYC Code of Ethics

The development of the NAEYC Code of Ethics began with a survey that confirmed members' desire for a code to guide ethical behavior. The next steps in the process involved identifying recurring ethical issues faced by early childhood educators and conducting workshops in which NAEYC members identified the core values of the early childhood field and worked through some of the issues that had been identified to determine what ethical early childhood educators should do. (For further information about the Code's history and development, see Appendix A.)

The Code consists of a preamble, a list of Core Values, and sections that address early childhood educators' ethical responsibilities to children, families, colleagues, and the community and society. It is accompanied by a commitment statement, which is not a part of the Code but a personal expression of resolve to uphold the values and responsibilities shared by all members of the field.

The Core Values included in the Code are deeply rooted in the history of early childhood education and express the field's central beliefs and its commitment to society. They are based on the literature of the early childhood field and the values expressed by participants in the ethics workshops conducted during the Code's development. These core values make it possible for early childhood educators to agree on ethical issues by moving from personal values to professional values that everyone in the field can embrace.

Each of the Code's four sections includes a brief introduction, a list of **Ideals,** and a list of **Principles.** The Ideals describe desirable, exemplary professional behavior. The Principles (sometimes referred to as rules of professional conduct) identify practices that are required, permitted, or prohibited and are designed to help early childhood educators distinguish between acceptable and unacceptable professional behavior.

> **?** What was your initial reaction to the NAEYC Code of Ethical Conduct? How have you used it in your work? In what ways have you found it helpful?

Supplements to the Code

NAEYC developed supplements to the Code to address the particular needs of two groups of early childhood educators. The Supplement for Early Childhood Adult Educators, adopted in 2004, is designed to provide ethical guidance for faculty at two- and four-year colleges and universities and others who provide training in non-credit-granting settings.

The Supplement for Early Childhood Program Administrators, adopted in 2006, addresses the particular ethical issues faced by those in administrative and supervisory roles (see pages 135–142). It provides guidance for addressing challenging issues that involve children, families, and colleagues as well as other stakeholders, such as employees, sponsoring agencies, and funders. Both supplements are designed to be used *with* the Code—they do not stand alone.

The Issue of Code Enforcement

A code of ethics can be viewed as part of the contract between the members of a profession and those they serve. For this reason, the codes of recognized professions like medicine and law have a mechanism for identifying ethical breaches and disciplining those who violate ethical standards. Currently there is no provision for enforcement of the NAEYC Code; NAEYC believes that the field of early childhood education is best served by focusing its efforts on disseminating the Code as widely as possible and encouraging its use by the membership rather than determining how it could be enforced.

Even a code that is not formally enforced can provide significant benefits to a professional group. As Marina Schwimmer and Bruce Maxwell (2017) observe, codes of ethics "reinforce public trust by setting forth explicitly and publicly the ethical standards that the public can expect a group of professionals to adhere to in their relationships with them ... [they are] a kind of pact between a group of professionals who provide an important public service ... and the people who rely on their services" (2).

> **?** What would be the advantages of enforcing the Code? Of having it be voluntary? Which do you think is preferable and why? Do you think a code can carry weight and remain voluntary?

The NAEYC Code of Ethical Conduct has been a valuable resource for many years. It has provided a unifying force in a field that is characterized by diversity in practitioner background, required training, and setting. Because of these differences, the Code addresses issues quite specifically. It lays out the aspirations of the early childhood field, makes it clear which professional behaviors are required and prohibited, and offers guidance in addressing some of the ethical issues that frequently occur. The Code outlines standards of behavior that, when they become part of every practitioner's repertoire, protect children and families and can lead to greater respect for those who work with them.

3

Addressing Ethical Issues

In your work, you are very likely to face situations that involve questions of morality and ethics. You may need to weigh competing obligations to children, families, colleagues, and your community and society or make a difficult or unpopular decision.

This chapter will help you sort through the following:

- Determine the nature of a workplace problem: Is it an issue of professional practice or an ethical issue?
- Determine the kind of ethical issue you are facing: Is it a responsibility or a dilemma?
- Engage in a thorough, systematic decision-making process that leads to an ethical course of action.

The NAEYC Code of Ethical Conduct can help you identify your responsibilities and guide your decision making when you encounter predicaments that involve ethics: considerations of right and wrong, rights and responsibilities, conflicting priorities, or human welfare. These ethical issues are apt to surface as you interact with children, families, coworkers, and community members. They may involve program decisions and might call on you to advocate for children in your community, state, or nation, such as in the Ineffective Child Protective Services Agency and Standardized Testing in Kindergarten cases in Chapter 7.

This chapter and the four that follow explore some of the ethical challenges you might encounter and identify how the Code can help answer this important question: "What should an ethical early childhood educator do?"

Ethical Responsibilities

Ethical responsibilities are mandates. They describe how you are required to act and what you must or must not do in situations that involve ethics. They are clearly spelled out in the Principles in the NAEYC Code. Following are some examples of these mandates.

Early childhood educators shall

> ... not harm children ... not participate in practices that are emotionally damaging, physically harmful, disrespectful, degrading, dangerous, exploitative, or intimidating to children (P-1.1)

> ... use appropriate assessment systems, which include multiple sources of information (P-1.5)

> ... not deny family members access to their child's classroom or program setting (P-2.1)

> ... make every effort to communicate effectively with all families in a language that they understand (P-2.5)

> ... maintain confidentiality and ... respect the family's right to privacy (P-2.13)

> ... not participate in practices that discriminate against a coworker because of sex, race, national origin, religious beliefs or other affiliations, age, marital status/family structure, disability, or sexual orientation (P-3A.4)

> ... be familiar with laws and regulations that serve to protect the children in our programs and be vigilant in ensuring that these laws and regulations are followed (P-4.6)

In addition to the responsibilities outlined in the Code, program administrators' responsibilities call on them to

> ... ensure that the programs we administer are safe and developmentally appropriate in accordance with standards of the field (P-1.2)

> ... develop enrollment policies that clearly describe admission policies and priorities (P-2.5)

> ... work to ensure that ongoing training is available and accessible (P-3.8)

> ... manage resources responsibly and accurately account for their use (P-4.3)

Accepting the responsibilities laid out in the Principles may mean that you must take an unpopular position, gather more information, or change practices that you are comfortable with. For example, you may need to challenge a director who has not taken steps to translate program materials for the Hmong families whose children have recently enrolled in her program. When you learn you have a responsibility to use multiple sources of information to appropriately assess children, you may decide to find an assessment that is more comprehensive than the checklist you've been using. If you are a program director, you may find you have an obligation to update your program's outdated staff manual so it accurately describes current policies and standards.

Think about how you might respond if, on the third rainy afternoon in a row, the children are restless and the teacher in the next room suggests that you show them a popular animated movie that the children in her group love. The movie offers no educational value.

This suggestion is tempting; the movie would occupy the children on an afternoon when they cannot go outside. However, deciding whether or not to let the children watch it is not an ethical dilemma. Showing the movie would be a violation of your ethical responsibilities to be familiar with the knowledge base of early childhood education and to provide worthwhile experiences for children. An ethical early childhood educator would instead get out tumbling mats or finger paints rather than show the movie.

Doing the right thing by honoring the responsibilities spelled out in the Code and supplements may not always be easy or popular. But to conscientiously embrace your profession's core values and ethical principles, your actions must demonstrate that you accept these responsibilities. One of the most important aspects of the Code is its affirmation of what is right—it defines the high road of ethical behavior.

> **?** Consider a workplace situation in which you were tempted to do what was easy or what others thought was acceptable rather than what you believed was right. What did you do? Were you able to keep sight of your responsibilities to all involved? How would you describe your thinking about it to someone new to the field?

Ethical Dilemmas

While some ethical issues are responsibilities for which the Code provides just one clear-cut course of action, others are **ethical dilemmas**— moral conflicts that involve determining how to act when an individual faces conflicting professional values and responsibilities. A dilemma is a situation for which there is more than one possible **resolution,** each of which can be justified in moral terms. A dilemma can be viewed as a situation that deals with two "rights" or sometimes two "wrongs."

Ethical dilemmas are different from other workplace problems in several ways:

- First, in an ethical dilemma, the legitimate needs and interests of one individual or group must give way to those of another individual or group. You must do something, and you must choose between two or more actions, each of which has both benefits and costs. This is why you sometimes hear the expression "on the horns of a dilemma," which refers to the two-pronged nature of these situations.
- Second, a dilemma may involve a conflict between two or more of the Core Values described in the Code. For example, when a 3-year-old's parents ask the director to move him to a class for 4-year-olds and his teachers feel that he is not ready, the director faces an ethical

The term *resolution* describes the course of action decided on through the systematic analysis of an ethical dilemma. It suggests that there is more than one morally acceptable response; if the first strategy you try does not resolve the dilemma, the next one you try might. We do not use the term *solution* when discussing appropriate responses to dilemmas because it suggests that there is only one correct way to handle a situation.

dilemma. The Ideal of maintaining a healthy setting that fosters children's development and the Principle that calls for early childhood educators not to do anything that might harm a child conflict with the Ideals of respecting his family's preferences and the importance of creating a partnership with them.

- Third, dilemmas rarely have simple answers. An ethical dilemma cannot be resolved by simply following the rules. In fact, you won't find easy resolutions to dilemmas in this or any other book. You can, however, learn to work through the process of making these difficult decisions by skillfully relying on the guidance provided by the Code.

Analyzing and Addressing Workplace Issues: A Framework

When you encounter an issue or problem, it is helpful to approach it using a multistep process. The following text and graphics describe this framework for addressing workplace problems.

Part I—Determine the Nature of the Problem

Is it an ethical issue? The first step to take when you encounter a workplace problem is to ask yourself, "Does it involve an issue of right or wrong, a duty or an obligation, human welfare, or individuals' best interests?" If you answer no, it is not an ethical issue (say, for example, another teacher often borrows supplies from you and does not return or replace them). You can handle these issues as you would any workplace concern. If you answer yes, however, you are facing an issue that involves ethics.

Is it a legal responsibility? If an ethical issue involves a legal responsibility, you must obey the law. The Suspected Child Abuse case in Chapter 4 and the Ineffective Child Protective Services Agency case in Chapter 7, both of which involved suspected child abuse, illustrate examples of legal responsibilities.

Is it an ethical responsibility or an ethical dilemma? If the issue involves ethics and is not a matter of law, ask yourself, "Is this an ethical responsibility or an ethical dilemma?" What you do next will depend on how you answer that question. As noted previously, ethical responsibilities are mandates that are clearly spelled out by the Principles of the NAEYC Code and that you must always honor. If you determine that a situation involves ethics but is not a clear-cut responsibility, you are probably facing an ethical dilemma.

The graphic on page 21 illustrates the essential first steps to take when analyzing and addressing any workplace issue.

Part II—Analyze the Ethical Dilemma

When you are facing an ethical dilemma, use the systematic process described in the pages that follow (and illustrated in the graphic on page 27) to help you decide on a defensible course of action. This process can be challenging because a dilemma puts the legitimate interests of one person or group in conflict with those of another person or group. This

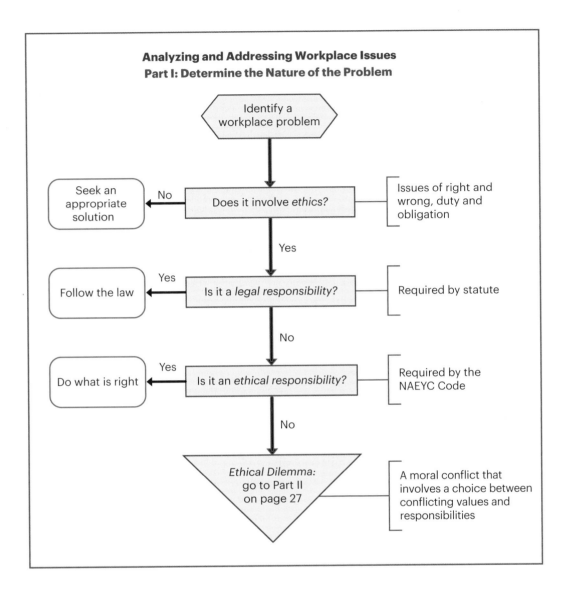

Analyzing and Addressing Workplace Issues
Part I: Determine the Nature of the Problem

Identify a workplace problem

Does it involve *ethics*? — Issues of right and wrong, duty and obligation

No → Seek an appropriate solution

Yes ↓

Is it a *legal responsibility*? — Required by statute

Yes → Follow the law

No ↓

Is it an *ethical responsibility*? — Required by the NAEYC Code

Yes → Do what is right

No ↓

Ethical Dilemma: go to Part II on page 27 — A moral conflict that involves a choice between conflicting values and responsibilities

might mean that you must consider whether to place the needs of a child or his parent first or whether to protect the rights of the group even if doing so limits the options of an individual child. Finding a resolution to an ethical dilemma requires balancing the interests, needs, and priorities of one person or group of individuals against those of another while trying to maintain positive relationships with everyone involved.

Some ethical dilemmas demand an immediate response. If an angry mother demands to know who bit her toddler, you need to respond on the spot. That doesn't mean, however, that your actions should be less intentional than if you had time to think through the request. It will be easier to respond under pressure in such situations if you are familiar with the Code, know that you have an ethical obligation to maintain confidentiality, and have had enough experience using the Code to respond in a way that feels like second nature.

More often when a situation arises, you will have time to think about what you should do. Sometimes it may be helpful to talk through the situation with a friend, one or more colleagues, your director, or your instructor, as the teacher did in the Personal Business case in Chapter 6 after her coteacher continually left the classroom to attend to personal business.

Understanding ethics and responding to situations in an ethical fashion are not instinctive. Resolving dilemmas is not easy; ethical decision making is a skill that must be learned. In his early writing about ethics for NAEYC, Kenneth Kipnis (1987) made this observation that is still applicable today:

> It is not easy to work one's way through dilemmas in professional ethics. The choices we face are painful, it is often unclear where help is to be found, and people disagree about what to do. Ethics, like mathematics, requires disciplined thought. But as with any practical way of approaching problems, it can be taught. There are useful definitions to be learned, ground rules for discussion, and strategies that can help us reach resolution. As with most skills—cooking, skiing, throwing a pot, and using a computer—ethics can be taught. (26)

The next few pages outline a process for resolving ethical dilemmas. The four chapters that follow demonstrate how to apply this decision-making process to examples of ethical dilemmas teachers and administrators face in their work.

1. Identify the Conflicting Responsibilities

The first step in resolving an ethical dilemma is to identify the conflicting values and responsibilities. This includes thinking about everyone who is involved (the stakeholders). What does each person or group need? What are your obligations to each? What values are in conflict? If it is clear that you need to make a choice between stakeholders, you are dealing with a true ethical dilemma. To make a morally justifiable decision, you need to weigh and balance your obligations to each stakeholder.

In The Nap case in Chapter 5, which involves a parent who wants the teacher to keep her 4-year-old from napping at school, the teacher must choose a course of action. Which Ideals and Principles in the Code will guide the teacher as she balances her responsibilities to the child and the parent? Whose interests should be given the greatest weight if she cannot find a compromise that works?

Upon reflection, the teacher recognizes that more than one right resolution is possible. In this situation, Ideals in the Code relating to children and families are in conflict with each other.

On the one hand, the teacher might decide to prevent the child from taking a nap, because she knows how hard it is for this mother to get to work in the morning and perform well on the job without having had a good night's sleep. If asked why she chose that course of action, she might say that she was guided by Ideal 2.6, which calls on her to respect families' wishes and honor their right to make decisions for their children.

On the other hand, the teacher might refuse to honor the mother's request and allow the child to nap with the other children. She could justify this decision with Ideal 1.5, which states that early childhood educators should strive to create safe and healthy settings that foster children's healthy development. She knows that most 4-year-olds need a nap after lunch, and she has observed that this child needs a nap in order to have a productive afternoon. Either decision can be justified, and each involves some benefits and some costs.

The conflicting obligations in a situation may be clearer if you summarize the choice between alternatives. You could think about The Nap case like this: "Should I do what I think is best for the child *or* should I honor the mother's request?"

> Have you ever faced a situation in which you had to choose between two justifiable alternatives? What were the competing interests? How did you respond? How did you determine the right thing to do?

2. Brainstorm Possible Resolutions

When you understand the conflicting values and responsibilities involved, brainstorm some possible responses to the situation. Generate ideas without analyzing them or rejecting any, and make a list of all the possible responses you can think of.

Next, consider the feasibility and fairness of each response. Some might be unreasonably harsh, like telling the mother no without considering what you could do to accommodate her request. Some might be morally indefensible, such as letting the child sleep and then telling him "You almost fell asleep" so his mother wouldn't know he had napped. Other possible responses may include courses of action that would resolve the problem without forcing you to make a difficult decision (see the next section on ethical finesse). And some may seem reasonable but would require you to give the needs of one stakeholder (the mother or the child) priority over those of the other. Consider each of the approaches and eliminate responses that are unacceptable so you can identify some courses of action you feel could be justified by relying on the Code.

3. Consider Ethical Finesse

When you are clear about the conflicting values and responsibilities and have brainstormed some possible responses to the situation, think about whether there is a way to use **ethical finesse**—a creative response to an ethical dilemma that meets the needs of everyone involved and allows the educator to avoid having to make a difficult decision. It is likely that many of the dilemmas you encounter can be addressed amicably by finesse. Compromising and negotiating without having to choose the needs of one party over the other is almost always the better route.

In the nap situation, could the teacher negotiate a resolution that meets *both* the parent's and the child's needs? The teacher could help the mother develop more effective bedtime routines for the child, or she could try letting the child take only a short nap. She could have him go to another classroom where children rest but do not sleep in the afternoon, or she and his mother might come up with some other arrangement that is acceptable to them both.

Ethical finesse can help alleviate many problems. In most situations, it is the first approach you will try, but it does not always resolve the problem. Understand your options and be prepared to make a difficult decision if your attempts at finesse are not feasible or successful.

4. Look for Guidance in the NAEYC Code

When you realize that a dilemma cannot be handled with finesse, turn to the Code to determine a morally defensible resolution and prepare to act. Begin by identifying which, if any, of the Code's Core Values apply to the situation. Core Values do not address every dilemma, but when they do, they will remind you that you should make every effort to honor these important foundational beliefs of the field.

After you consider the Core Values, carefully review all of the Code's Ideals and Principles. They are based on the Core Values but offer more specific guidance and will help clarify your obligations. It is important to review the entire Code because some situations are addressed in several sections, as you will see in the analyses of several cases in the chapters that follow. This process will help you prioritize the conflicting values and responsibilities that make this situation an ethical dilemma. It may be helpful to list all the items related to the situation you are facing.

Next, ask yourself if you have all of the information you need to resolve the problem. Check the accuracy of your information or gather additional facts by talking with and observing children and by talking with families, staff members, or specialists who have relevant expertise. Depending on the situation, you may also want to review school or center policies, as the teacher did in the No Hugging case in Chapter 6 when her principal told the staff not to hug students or use any physical affection.

Finally, decide how to best prioritize the relevant items in the Code, come up with one or more resolutions that you believe are justifiable, and consider the costs and benefits of each alternative before you make a decision.

5. Decide on a Justifiable Course of Action

You can draw on a number of resources as you weigh the alternative resolutions for an ethical dilemma:

- Your personal values and morality
- The Core Values and ethical guidance of your profession expressed in the Ideals and Principles of the Code

- The wisdom that comes from the historical traditions of moral philosophy (see the box on page 26)
- The insights of colleagues you have consulted
- Your own best judgment

It takes courage to make a difficult decision and stick to it. Carefully considering the alternatives in combination with guidance from the field and your own best judgment should lead you to a sound decision that you could justify by referring to the NAEYC Code if asked to do so.

Remember that while there may be a number of acceptable resolutions to an ethical dilemma, there also are unacceptable alternatives. If that were not the case, there would be little point in studying ethics. We hope this book will help you determine well-reasoned, ethically supportable resolutions to the ethical issues you encounter in your work and avoid indefensible responses that violate the trust of children, families, colleagues, or the community.

Implement Your Resolution and Reflect

Ultimately you are closest to the situation. You need to be prepared to use all of the available resources to decide which resolution is best for the particular circumstances you are facing, to be responsible for making a defensible decision, and to take appropriate action. But deciding what to do is not the end of the process. In most cases, you will need to inform stakeholders who are not going to have their wishes or needs accommodated because of the decision you have made. It can be particularly challenging to disappoint a colleague, a friend, or a member of a child's family with whom you have a good relationship. Communicate your decision diplomatically, openly, and honestly, and encourage all involved to listen to each other with care and courtesy (Feeney, Freeman, & Moravcik 2016). After implementing the decision, look at the success of the outcome and reflect on the process you used to reach this resolution to see what you learned from it.

As you work your way through a dilemma, you may find that it has implications for policy in your program or your community. Sometimes you will realize that the issue could have been avoided or that it would have been much easier to resolve if an appropriate policy had been in place. The Teacher Talk case in Chapter 6, in which a teacher's colleague is sharing confidential information about a family with other school staff, illustrates this. In such cases, work with colleagues to consider how you might develop new policies or revise old ones that would help to prevent the need to address this kind of difficult-to-resolve dilemma in the future.

At times you may realize that your community needs policies to better protect the interests of children and their families. Because early childhood professionals have a responsibility to stand up and be heard in the public policy arena, you might consider addressing an issue you care about in your community that is of concern to you. The policy implications of several commonly occurring ethical dilemmas are included in the chapters that follow.

Applying Theories of Moral Philosophy

Philosophers and others who study morality and ethics describe several approaches to evaluating responses to ethical issues. The following briefly summarizes three traditions of moral philosophy and accompanying principles for deliberating about dilemmas. Each provides a different lens to help you evaluate resolutions to ethical dilemmas (Freeman & Feeney 2016; Kidder 2009).

Utilitarianism. Based on the nineteenth-century writings of British philosophers Jeremy Bentham and John Stuart Mill, *utilitarianism* (sometimes called *consequentialism*) can be summarized by the advice to "do what's best for the greatest number of people" (Kidder 2009, 152). Philosophers who embrace this approach maintain that the best action is the one that benefits the most people and would result in the most good (Driver 2014). A question that illustrates utilitarian thinking is "Does this decision help more people than it hurts?"

Critics of utilitarianism insist that it is impossible to foresee the consequences of an action and that even if a large number of people would benefit from an action, others may be hurt by it. What's more, it is very difficult for an individual who has a stake in the outcome of a difficult situation to be impartial about identifying the best resolution (Frey 2013). Of course, the field of early childhood education is often concerned with ensuring that the rights and privileges of the majority do not infringe on the rights of minority groups—which is consistent with the Code's Core Values and a number of its Ideals and Principles.

The rightness of an action. Another tradition of moral philosophy is based on the writings of Immanuel Kant, an eighteenth-century German philosopher. He described "categorical imperatives," absolute and unconditional principles individuals must always follow. His focus was on the *rightness* of a person's actions, not the consequences of those actions. Philosophers from this school believe that individuals should act rationally and in such a way that their actions could become universal standards that everyone should follow. They believe that acting this way creates the greatest good because it promotes actions that are universally acceptable.

The philosophical principle based on this approach is to "follow your highest sense of principle" (Kidder 2009, 152). The following two questions illustrate how Kant's approach to moral philosophy might apply to early childhood educators: "Is this the way I think all early childhood educators should act?" and "Is this action the best one for the field as a whole?"

Critics suggest that demanding that everyone always follow the same philosophical principles is impossibly strict and would thwart creativity and individualism. In addition, generally accepted principles can conflict with each other (Hill 2013; Johnson & Cureton 2016; Kidder 2009).

Ethic of care. The third philosophical approach is consistent with ideas about women's morality that have been described by Nel Noddings (1984) and Carol Gilligan (1993). It is often referred to as the *ethic of care* or *feminist ethics*. This tradition advises individuals to evaluate their actions based on the extent to which they promote the interests of others and preserve the fabric of relationships. It is often associated with Christianity but can in fact be found in the doctrines of all major religions (Jaggar 2013; Tong & Williams 2009). Critics note that this approach doesn't give direct guidance to individuals trying to make difficult ethical choices.

"Do unto others as you would have others do unto you" is familiar advice with roots in this philosophical tradition of caring (Kidder 2009). As you consider this philosophical perspective, you might ask yourself, "Is this the way I would want others to treat me?" and "Is this resolution respectful of people and relationships?"

Considering ethical guidance from these three schools of thought may be a useful way to think about the impact of the resolutions to dilemmas you are pondering. They can give you a better understanding of the consequences of your actions and help you develop a well-reasoned rationale. You can further reflect on the validity of a proposed resolution by asking yourself, "Could I justify this decision to the community at large if a news reporter asked me to?"

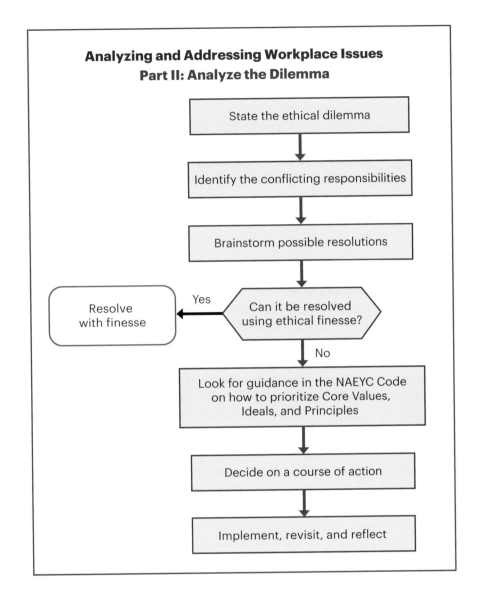

Analyzing and Addressing Workplace Issues
Part II: Analyze the Dilemma

State the ethical dilemma

Identify the conflicting responsibilities

Brainstorm possible resolutions

Can it be resolved using ethical finesse? — Yes → Resolve with finesse

No

Look for guidance in the NAEYC Code on how to prioritize Core Values, Ideals, and Principles

Decide on a course of action

Implement, revisit, and reflect

Advice About Difficult Dilemmas

Regardless of your past experience or your understanding of ethics, you may find it helpful to talk over a difficult issue with someone whose opinion you respect. Find someone who can offer an objective critique and is willing to tell you if she thinks your view is flawed. She may affirm that your inclinations are correct or offer insights you may have overlooked. Don't ask for advice from someone you know will simply agree with you; a rubber stamp for your own ideas will not help you find the best, most ethical resolution.

If the problem has a legal dimension, such as a difficult hiring or termination decision, you may want to discuss it informally with a lawyer—perhaps a member of your program's board or someone you know in the community. A lawyer's informal advice may be useful as you try to sort out the legal aspects of the issue, and it may be all the consultation you need.

For larger, more serious problems, you may need to formally retain legal counsel to reach a final resolution to the problem. In that case, the lawyer's advice and recommendations may later serve to explain or justify your good faith efforts and actions if they are challenged.

> **?** Think about a time you made a difficult decision as you addressed an ethical dilemma. Who were the stakeholders, and what were your obligations to each? What resources did you use to help you resolve the dilemma? What was the outcome?

Your Stage of Professional Development and Ethical Issues

The way you approach moral issues in your work depends on your stage of professional development and your life experiences. When you are new to your position, just learning to teach a group of children or work with staff and families, you begin your ethics journey by learning to recognize ethical issues and understand the difference between legal and ethical responsibilities and ethical dilemmas. When you are clear about those distinctions, you are ready to begin using the decision-making process described on pages 20–25 to reach defensible resolutions to ethical dilemmas. You may need the support of a more experienced colleague, mentor, or program director to take an unpopular or controversial position.

In time, you will become more skilled in ethical analysis and more comfortable making a principled but potentially unpopular decision. You may also be better able to explain the rationale behind that decision by relying on the Code.

And when you are a veteran in the field with many years of experience, you may find it helpful to consider your decision in terms of the three theories of moral philosophy described earlier. You may even be ready to teach others about the Code and how to implement it (Feeney, Freeman, & Moravcik 2016).

Many who are beginning their careers are inclined to evaluate possible responses by considering the immediate consequences of an action. As they grow in experience, they develop the ability to address ethical issues by considering the universal principles of justice, rights, equality, and human welfare (Feeney, Freeman, & Moravcik 2016).

How Ethical Dilemmas Are Presented in this Book

The next four chapters correspond to the four sections of the NAEYC Code: early childhood educators' responsibilities to children, families, colleagues, and community and society. Each chapter discusses ethical responsibilities relative to a particular section of the Code and provides in-depth studies of dilemmas that are based on real-life situations that teachers, caregivers, and administrators have faced. The stories have been adapted for use in this book, and fictitious names are used for all involved.

The four parts of the Code address different professional relationships. However, in real life the distinctions between these relationships are not clear cut. Ethical responsibilities in one area intersect and overlap with responsibilities in the others. Your obligations to children are related to your responsibilities to families, and your relationships with colleagues and the community relate to your responsibilities to children and their families. Each case presented in these chapters focuses on the primary relationship involved. Together, they illustrate the kinds of ethical issues early childhood educators are apt to encounter in their work.

The analysis of each case shows how the collective wisdom and expert guidance of experienced colleagues, expressed in NAEYC's ethical code, can help you resolve the real-life dilemmas of your own workplace. The Core Values, Ideals, and Principles embraced by like-minded professionals can become guideposts in your work with young children and their families.

Although the scenarios presented in the next chapters are real, their analysis is based on the limited information that was shared with us, the authors. If you encounter a dilemma similar to one you read about here, remember that every situation is different. You will need to conduct your own analysis to find the resolution that best fits your specific circumstances.

That means your task will be easier in some ways, and more difficult in others, than the process of analysis described in the chapters that follow. You will have much more information than is presented here, but you are likely to be facing several concerned stakeholders and a potentially stressful and high-stakes situation.

As you think about addressing the ethical dilemmas you encounter in your work, keep in mind that the resolutions we describe are not the only possible "right" answers. Our purpose is to model the decision-making process you can use to find sound resolutions to the dilemmas you face.

4

Ethical Responsibilities to Children

Childhood is a unique and valuable stage in the human life cycle. Our paramount responsibility is to provide care and education in settings that are safe, healthy, nurturing, and responsive for each child. We are committed to supporting children's development and learning; respecting individual differences; and helping children learn to live, play, and work cooperatively. We are also committed to promoting children's self-awareness, competence, self-worth, resiliency, and physical well-being.

—NAEYC Code of Ethical Conduct

NAEYC describes itself as "a professional membership organization that works to promote high-quality early learning for all young children, birth through age 8, by connecting early childhood practice, policy, and research" (NAEYC 2017). The association's mission is to promote "high-quality early learning for all children, birth through age 8, by connecting practice, policy, and research … and advance a diverse, dynamic early childhood profession and support all who care for, educate, and work on behalf of young children." Its vision is that "all young children thrive and learn in a society dedicated to ensuring they reach their full potential" (NAEYC 2017). These statements, along with the Core Values that provide a foundation for the NAEYC Code of Ethical Conduct, demonstrate why it is fitting that the Code begins by addressing our first and most important responsibility: to ensure children's well-being.

This chapter focuses on early childhood educators' responsibilities to children as they are addressed in the first section of the NAEYC Code. However, the entire Code, including the sections addressing responsibilities to families, colleagues, and community and society, is designed to guide your daily interactions with young children and their families and outline your role in supporting children's healthy growth and development. While not all of the ethical situations in this book relate directly to children, the guidance is intended to help you think systematically about your work with children and how you can balance their needs and your responsibilities to them with your professional responsibilities to families, colleagues, and community and society.

As noted in Chapter 2, a tremendous imbalance of power exists between early childhood educators and the children in their care, and children are quite defenseless against harmful practices. For these reasons, it is extremely important that you know and abide by the safeguards for children that are part of the Code.

Ideals

The 12 Ideals in the first section of the Code point individuals in the direction of desirable and exemplary professional behavior in their work with children (see page 129 in Appendix B). They cover such topics as being knowledgeable about child development and appropriate educational practices, respecting the uniqueness of each child and meeting the needs of all children, using assessment appropriately, and working with families through transitions.

The first section of the administrator supplement establishes that administrators' first responsibility is to ensure that the programs they lead are "safe, heathy, nurturing, and responsive to each child" (NAEYC 2011). While children's well-being is the administrators' first priority, the supplement underscores the additional responsibility to support families' essential role in promoting their children's development. The first section of the administrator supplement contains two Ideals: ensuring that decisions are based on children's needs and providing a high-quality program based on sound child development principles and best practices (see page 137 in Appendix C).

Principles

Eleven Principles (or rules of professional conduct) pertain to responsibilities to children (see pages 129–130 in Appendix B). They provide guidance and identify practices that are required, permitted, or prohibited on topics that include educational supports and services, discrimination, and suspected child abuse or neglect. Most important—as noted in the first Principle, which has precedence over all others in the Code—early childhood educators shall not harm children.

The administrator supplement contains several Principles related to administrators' responsibilities toward children (see page 137–138 in Appendix C). These address such issues as having clearly stated policies about respectful treatment of children and families, applying policies fairly, and advocating for the well-being of children and families.

Typical Issues Involving Ethical Responsibilities to Children

This chapter addresses two kinds of ethical issues that focus primarily on children.

Balancing the Needs of an Individual Child with the Needs of the Group

These situations challenge teachers to find resolutions that take into account their responsibilities to *all* of the children in their care—those who demand a great deal of attention and those who may be overlooked as a result. These issues also involve educators' responsibilities to themselves and to their colleagues. The first two cases in this chapter present two variations of a dilemma teachers face when they must balance their responsibilities to individual children with their responsibilities to a whole group of children.

Situations that Involve Suspected Child Abuse or Neglect

Early childhood educators sometimes encounter situations in which they suspect a child's safety and well-being are endangered by abuse or neglect. These situations involve both adults and children, but because the primary focus in these situations is the welfare of the child, we address abuse in this chapter (see also the Ineffective Child Protective Services Agency case in Chapter 7).

Implicit bias reflects "attitudes or stereotypes that affect our understanding, actions, and decisions in an unconscious manner" (Staats et al. 2015, 62). Such bias can unintentionally lead to unfair or unjust treatment of some children, families, and colleagues. As you read the examples in this book and wrestle with ethical questions in your own work, consider how factors such as culture, race and ethnicity, gender, socioeconomic status, and differing abilities affect your perception of and interactions with children and your ability to treat all children and families equitably. When you make decisions as to what is right and fair, consider the question "What biases may be influencing this decision that could have a negative impact on the child, the family, or a colleague?"

Case 1: Child with Aggressive Behavior

Parker, a 4-year-old who attends a community-based early education and care program, is physically large for his age and tends to be extremely aggressive. His behavior frightens and sometimes hurts the other children. His teacher, Rayna, has repeatedly discussed his behavior with the center director, who is sympathetic but has been unable to help. Parker's parents have heard Rayna's concerns, but because they feel that his behavior is typical for boys his age, they won't seek counseling. A preschool specialist from the Department of Mental Health has observed the child and suggested some techniques to try, but none of her recommendations have helped. The other parents are starting to complain to Rayna because Parker's behavior intimidates their children. She is becoming stressed and tired, and her patience is wearing thin. Rayna and her coteacher spend so much time trying to handle Parker's behavior that they feel they are not able to give the other children the attention they need and deserve.

Parker's story is familiar to many educators and a good place to begin discussing the kinds of ethical dilemmas you are likely to encounter in your work. In fact, whenever we, the authors of this book, conduct ethics workshops, we almost always hear participants say that they have worked with a child like Parker. Some of the most dramatic moments in these workshops occur when teachers share the wrenching decisions they have had to make when dealing with a child who was aggressive or who in some other way required an inordinate amount of their time and attention.

Determine the Nature of the Problem

Rayna faces an ethical issue because this situation involves her responsibilities both to Parker and to his classmates. It puts her in the position of having to consider how she will meet the needs of all of the children in her group. It involves ethics because it can be argued that it is right to honor Parker's need for a positive preschool experience and also right for the other children in the class to be safe and to feel secure in school.

Rayna realizes she is facing an ethical dilemma rather than an ethical responsibility; there is no clear-cut course of action. She must weigh and balance her conflicting responsibilities to Parker and his family with those to the other children in the group and their families. Each of these obligations is legitimate, yet if it is not possible to successfully honor them all, Rayna will need to choose between opposing but defensible claims on her time and attention.

Next, Rayna follows the steps to analyze her situation and reach a justifiable resolution.

1. Identify the Conflicting Responsibilities

Rayna believes in Parker's right to attend school with his peers and to have a positive experience there. She knows his behavior needs to be responded to appropriately, and she would like his teachers and classmates to value him as a member of the class.

She also knows that the other children in the group need to be safe, and she has observed that they frequently need an adult to protect them from potentially harmful interactions with Parker. She believes she has a responsibility to be Parker's advocate and to help him become successful in school, but his behavior is isolating him and is becoming increasingly stressful for her. She must balance the needs of the entire class with Parker's right to participate in the program.

Rayna knows she also has obligations to the families of all the children in her care. Parker's family should have access to a program that can meet their son's needs. The families of the other children are entitled to know that their children can have a positive experience and that they are not being threatened with injury.

This situation also raises issues related to Parker's teachers' morale and their ability to perform their jobs well. Rayna is beginning to feel burned out, and her coteacher is experiencing similar feelings of fatigue. If Parker's outbursts and aggressive behaviors continue, it is possible that one or both of his teachers will resign in frustration to avoid remaining in a position where they are unable to meet the needs of all of the children. That would be a great loss to the program, and the children would miss these talented teachers.

2. Brainstorm Possible Resolutions

The possible resolutions to this dilemma are fairly obvious. Rayna and her colleague realize that they can continue to do the best they can with Parker using all of the resources available to them, or they can take the severe step of helping the family find another program that is better able to meet Parker's needs.

> **Have you ever been in a situation when the needs of an individual child made it difficult to attend to the needs of the other children in a group? What did you do? What resources did you use to help you address the issue?**

3. Consider Ethical Finesse

In Chapter 3 we defined *ethical finesse* as a strategy for solving ethical dilemmas through skillful handling that allows the teacher to avoid choosing between conflicting responsibilities. The situation involving Parker may lend itself to finessing. Before deciding to refer the family to another program, Rayna vows to try everything in her power to help Parker build the skills he needs to function successfully in the group. She identifies approaches that she has used successfully with other children and does some additional reading on child guidance.

Armed with these tools, Rayna tries several strategies. She pays special attention to being both gentle and firm with Parker, depending on his needs at the moment. She talks with Parker about how his outbursts affect the other children, and she encourages his classmates to express their feelings to him directly when he hurts or frightens them. When a child has had a frightening experience with Parker, she gives attention and support to the child who has been hurt. She tries pairing Parker with another child who can model appropriate prosocial behavior. She observes Parker's play carefully to learn to predict what triggers his aggressive behavior so that she can help prevent it or, when outbursts occur, redirect his energies before he injures a classmate. She reinforces Parker's positive interactions while showing him appropriate ways to express his anger and frustration.

Rayna also experiments with making changes to the classroom learning environment, transitions, routines, and the daily schedule to provide more structure for Parker. She modifies the curriculum to try making it a better match to Parker's abilities and interests.

When none of these efforts significantly improve his behavior, she works with her director to place him in another classroom for a week to see if a different setting, teachers, and group of children will have a positive effect.

Rayna arranges frequent conferences with Parker's parents to discuss his progress. She uses these opportunities to ask whether his behavior at school is markedly different from his behavior at home and to determine whether there are extraordinary stressors or medical conditions that could be causing his outbursts.

Rayna doesn't expect every child to fit the same mold, but based on her professional knowledge and experience, it is clear to her that Parker's behavior is not typical of 4-year-olds. Because his parents do not agree that his behavior requires out-of-the-ordinary intervention, she provides them with information on child development and arranges for them to observe in her classroom to see for themselves how Parker interacts with his peers and how the other 4-year-olds behave in the group setting. Rayna hopes that these efforts will help the parents realize that his present behavior is not typical. She wants to make them partners in her efforts to help Parker learn to deal more constructively with his feelings.

Rayna's director also arranges for a consultation with a specialist who helps her implement classroom-based interventions designed to modify Parker's behavior. These actions are all efforts at solving the problem without having to remove the child from the classroom or school.

4. Look for Guidance in the NAEYC Code

Once it has become clear to Rayna that the issues created by Parker's aggressive behavior are not going to be resolved with ethical finesse, she accepts the fact that she will have to take action. She now turns to the NAEYC Code for guidance in resolving this dilemma.

First, she reviews the Code's Core Values, but she does not think any relate directly to this situation. Next, she turns to the Code's Ideals, paying particular attention to the responsibilities she has to children. She notes the following Ideals that are relevant to the situation she is facing:

> I-1.2—To base program practices upon current knowledge and research in the field of early childhood education, child development, and related disciplines, as well as on particular knowledge of each child.
>
> I-1.3—To recognize and respect the unique qualities, abilities, and potential of each child.
>
> I-1.4—To appreciate the vulnerability of children and their dependence on adults.
>
> I-1.5—To create and maintain safe and healthy settings that foster children's social, emotional, cognitive, and physical development and that respect their dignity and their contributions.

I-1.8—To support the right of each child to play and learn in an inclusive environment that meets the needs of children with and without disabilities.

I-1.9—To advocate for and ensure that all children, including those with special needs, have access to the support services needed to be successful.

She also looks at the Ideals that relate to her responsibilities to families, in Section II:

I-2.2—To develop relationships of mutual trust and create partnerships with the families we serve.

I-2.4—To listen to families, acknowledge and build upon their strengths and competencies, and learn from families as we support them in their task of nurturing children.

I-2.6—To acknowledge families' childrearing values and their right to make decisions for their children.

I-2.7—To share information about each child's education and development with families and to help them understand and appreciate the current knowledge base of the early childhood profession.

I-2.8—To help family members enhance their understanding of their children, as staff are enhancing their understanding of each child through communications with families, and support family members in the continuing development of their skills as parents.

She then identifies these relevant Principles in the section addressing ethical responsibilities to children:

P-1.1—Above all, we shall not harm children. We shall not participate in practices that are emotionally damaging, physically harmful, disrespectful, degrading, dangerous, exploitative, or intimidating to children. **This principle has precedence over all others in this Code.**

P-1.2—We shall care for and educate children in positive emotional and social environments.

P-1.3—We shall not participate in practices that discriminate against children by denying benefits, giving special advantages, or excluding them from programs or activities.

P-1.4—We shall use two-way communications to involve all those with relevant knowledge (including families and staff) in decisions concerning a child, as appropriate, ensuring confidentiality of sensitive information.

P-1.7—We shall strive to build individual relationships with each child; make individualized adaptations in teaching strategies, learning environments, and curricula; and consult with the family so that each child benefits from the program. ... We shall collaborate with the child's family and appropriate specialists to determine the additional services needed and/or the placement option(s) most likely to ensure the child's success.

These items related to Rayna's ethical responsibilities to families also prove helpful as she works to develop a plan of action:

> P-2.4—We shall ensure that the family is involved in significant decisions affecting their child.

> P-2.9—We shall inform the family of injuries and incidents involving their child ... and of occurrences that might result in emotional stress.

> P-2.15—We shall be familiar with and appropriately refer families to community resources and professional support services. After a referral has been made, we shall follow up to ensure that services have been appropriately provided.

Parker's aggressive behavior has persisted in spite of the extraordinary amount of time and energy that Rayna and other members of the staff have devoted to helping him learn to control his behavior. Based on her professional knowledge and experience, she finally concludes that she cannot ensure the safety of the other children.

As Rayna continues to study the Code for guidance, she realizes that she has a professional responsibility to remind families that there are limits to the services her program can provide, an issue that is addressed in this item identifying her ethical responsibilities to the community and society:

> P-4.1—We shall communicate openly and truthfully about the nature and extent of services that we provide.

Rayna finds an additional relevant item:

> P-4.2—We shall apply for, accept, and work in positions for which we are personally well-suited and professionally qualified. We shall not offer services that we do not have the competence, qualifications, or resources to provide.

This Principle helps her better understand why her efforts to meet Parker's needs have been unsuccessful—she does not have specialized training in working with children who have severe emotional needs.

5. Decide on a Justifiable Course of Action

After trying several approaches to changing Parker's behavior, carefully reflecting on her professional skills and expertise, and considering the needs of all the children in her group, Rayna realizes she must make the safety and security of the other children in the group her highest priority. She decides that Parker should be removed from her classroom until the family has taken appropriate remedial steps. As a last resort alternative, this decision is supported by the Code, particularly P-1.7.

Before taking the drastic step of excluding Parker from the program, Rayna meets again with her program director to share her careful documentation of Parker's behavior in the classroom and to discuss the best way to present this decision to the family. They schedule a meeting with Parker's parents to describe the interventions they have tried and the lack of improvement in his behavior and to tell them that Parker may remain in the program only if the family receives counseling and provides for appropriate assistance in the classroom. They tell the family that if they are unwilling to pursue this course of action, the staff will help them find a more suitable program. Rayna and the director hope that as a result of this discussion Parker's parents will realize that his behavior is not typical for a 4-year-old and will agree to obtain help for him.

> **Do you believe that the decision to insist that Parker's family access specialized services or find another setting for him is justified?**

This case analysis is based on the assumption that Parker attends a private preschool program. These community settings are not likely to have access to special education services, and the teachers generally do not have specialized training in working with children with serious emotional needs. If Parker were attending a Head Start or public school program, Rayna's efforts would most likely revolve around making sure that his parents understand and acknowledge his special needs and working within the system to secure an evaluation and appropriate services for him.

Think About this Ethical Dilemma

Parker's story demonstrates the difficult balance that early childhood educators must achieve to meet the needs of all of the children in their care. Sometimes teachers of young children need to acknowledge that they cannot solve every problem and cannot be all things to all people.

However, asking a child to leave a program is a decision that should not be taken lightly. Teachers and administrators should use the systematic procedure described in this book to address ethical issues when considering whether or not a child should be excluded from a program. NAEYC and the professionals from the Division for Early Childhood of the Council for Exceptional Children worked hard to craft item P-1.7 in the NAEYC Code to provide ethical guidance that balances the rights of the individual with those of the larger group. The goal is that programs should make every effort to help children succeed in school. In the rare cases in which children cannot be served in their current program, they should be referred to programs that can meet their particular needs, not expelled.

Policy Implications

Research documents the prevalence of unjustified expulsions from preschools, including some that seem to have been enforced quite arbitrarily when a child demonstrated behavior that was well within developmental norms (Gilliam et al. 2016). NAEYC, the US Department of Health and Human Services (HHS), and the US Department of Education (ED) have engaged in efforts to raise the field's awareness of unreasonable expulsions and to prevent them. The joint HHS/ED "Policy Statement on Expulsion and Suspension Policies in Early Childhood Settings" contributes to these efforts by pointing out the negative effects of suspension and expulsion, including their impact on children's development, health, and future educational success (HHS & ED 2014).

Case 2: Child with Emotional and Behavioral Issues

Three-year-old Niani's play is limited to rolling a truck alongside the block area. During music time she howls, disrupting the activity. At naptime she bangs her head on the wall to put herself to sleep. Niani's parents have told her pediatrician about the concerns raised by Niani's teacher, Shana, and school staff. To their relief, Niani's doctor has assured her parents that Niani will outgrow this behavior. Shana and her assistant find that the class runs more smoothly, especially during group activities and naptime, if one teacher is always with Niani. Now another child's family is upset, complaining that Niani disturbs her child and keeps Shana and her assistant from paying attention to all of the children.

> **What is your first reaction to this situation? To whom does Shana have conflicting obligations? What factors should she consider as she decides what she should do? How might she address this issue?**

Niani's case is similar to Parker's. In both instances, the teachers must consider how to ensure that all children have the opportunity to fully participate in a program that supports their development and learning. In both of these situations, teachers are faced with balancing their responsibilities to the group with those to an individual child. They must also grapple with their obligations to the families of all of the children in their classrooms and to other staff, who feel ill-prepared to meet a particular child's needs while working effectively with the entire group.

Determine the Nature of the Problem

This case involves ethics because Shana knows that it would be right both to continue to work hard to try to meet Niani's needs and to refuse to include her if she does not receive services that will allow her teachers to focus on working with all the children in the group.

The situation Shana faces is an ethical dilemma; she realizes that it is not possible to do her best for the other children when Niani disturbs activities and requires almost constant one-to-one attention. She wants to provide a quality program for Niani, but this involves helping her family recognize that her behavior is extreme and requires specialized intervention. In addition, she sympathizes with the concerns expressed by the family who feels Niani is too disruptive and is taking too much of the teachers' time.

Preschool is often the first place where families of children with potential delays or disabilities come into regular contact with other children. Shana knows this and is sensitive to the fact that Niani's family may have deep-seated fears about their child's development. Their doctor temporarily relieved them of their anxieties, so it's not easy for them to accept Shana's recommendation that they get another opinion.

It is particularly difficult for an early childhood educator to disagree with a family's pediatrician. For many families, a doctor is ranked higher on the ladder of professional status than their child's preschool teacher, and the doctor's advice is more likely to hold sway. But in this case, it is important that Shana effectively communicate her concerns based on her own specialized professional knowledge.

While these cases are similar, it is useful to consider how they differ. Parker's teacher believes he could be successful in school if he learned to channel his energy and control his aggression. Shana knows that Niani's behaviors—playing exclusively with a single toy in a repetitive, ritualistic way; banging her head on the wall as a way to fall asleep; and howling during group music time—are all cause for concern.

1. Identify the Conflicting Responsibilities

The conflicting responsibilities are the same as those in the previous case. Shana has a responsibility to Niani and to the other children in her group who need her attention, as well as to all of the families involved. And she has a responsibility to herself and her colleagues to not become too stressed by dealing with a child whose needs require a great deal of adult attention.

2. Brainstorm Possible Resolutions

Like Rayna, Shana wants to create and maintain a safe, healthy setting that fosters the development of all the children. And, like Rayna, Shana needs to seriously consider the effect that one child is having on the other children in her class.

The alternatives are also similar to those in the previous dilemma. The teachers can manage to work with the child as best they can, or they can ask the family to find a more appropriate setting for their child.

3. Consider Ethical Finesse

Shana asks Niani's parents to observe in her classroom, thinking that they may have limited experience with young children and could benefit from spending time with Niani's classmates. Shana believes that they will see how different Niani's behavior is from that of her peers. She hopes that as a result of this experience they will agree to seek advice from a specialist in behavioral and emotional disorders.

If Niani's parents are able to recognize the problem and to begin the process of developing a specialized plan for intervention, Shana and her assistant can partner with the appropriate therapists to successfully finesse this dilemma. However, if this strategy is not successful, Shana must make a difficult decision.

4. Look for Guidance in the NAEYC Code

The items in the Code guiding Shana's considerations of how to deal with Niani and her family are the same as those that guided Rayna as she worked with Parker. In this instance, however, Shana's concern that she does not have specialized training that prepares her to work successfully with children with behavioral and emotional disorders is paramount. She begins her analysis of this dilemma by referring to P-4.1 and P-4.2:

> P-4.1—We shall communicate openly and truthfully about the nature and extent of services that we provide.

> P-4.2—We shall apply for, accept, and work in positions for which we are personally well-suited and professionally qualified. We shall not offer services that we do not have the competence, qualifications, or resources to provide.

She finds additional guidance in the Core Values, Ideals, and Principles identified in the discussion of Parker's behavior. Two Ideals encourage educators to appreciate each child's uniqueness and young children's vulnerability (see I-1.3 and I-1.4), but Shana realizes that the current situation is diminishing the quality of the educational experience for the rest of the children in her group (see I-1.5).

> I-1.3—To recognize and respect the unique qualities, abilities, and potential of each child.

> I-1.4—To appreciate the vulnerability of children and their dependence on adults.

> I-1.5—To create and maintain safe and healthy settings that foster children's social, emotional, cognitive, and physical development and that respect their dignity and their contributions.

Shana, and other staff in the school, must be sensitive to maintaining their trusting relationship with the family (I-2.2), but the reality is that Niani is not currently benefiting from this program. They realize that they have a responsibility to "advocate for and ensure that all children, including those with special needs, have access to the support services needed to be successful" (I-1.9).

As Shana continues to consult the Code, she notes an item pertaining to families that directs teachers

> I-2.2—To develop relationships of mutual trust and create partnerships with the families we serve.

Shana knows that early intervention is important for children who have severe emotional problems, so she focuses on her responsibility to do everything she can to ensure that Niani has access to appropriate interventions as soon as possible. Shana notes that other items in the Code can help her think about this situation. She realizes that she needs to collaborate with special educators to help the child's family access community resources that will address their child's needs.

> P-2.15—We shall be familiar with and appropriately refer families to community resources and professional support services. After a referral has been made, we shall follow up to ensure that services have been appropriately provided.

> I-4.2—To promote cooperation among professionals and agencies and interdisciplinary collaboration among professions concerned with addressing issues in the health, education, and well-being of young children, their families, and their early childhood educators.

One Principle in the NAEYC Code calls for Shana's particularly careful consideration. It directs early childhood educators to make every effort to maximize the potential of the child to benefit from a program, but allows that "if after such efforts have been exhausted, the current placement does not meet a child's needs, or the child is seriously jeopardizing the ability of other children to benefit from the program, we shall collaborate with the child's family and appropriate specialists to determine the additional services needed and/or the placement option(s) most likely to ensure the child's success" (P-1.7).

5. Decide on a Justifiable Course of Action

At first Shana was determined to keep Niani in her classroom, but she realizes that she and her assistant lack the knowledge and specialized skills required to meet the child's needs and those of the other children. She focuses her attention on providing the family the information and assistance they need.

Shana and her director meet again with the family to discuss the situation. They share their detailed observations of Niani and their concern for her welfare if she doesn't receive services in a timely manner. They offer to help the family have Niani evaluated and access the appropriate services. They tell the family that if they follow through, Niani may stay in the program until the evaluation is completed and arrangements have been made to implement needed interventions.

The school staff make it clear that, if the family does not agree to an evaluation for Niani, their only option is to help them find another placement. They hope, however, that this discussion will convince the family to seek appropriate help. They believe that there is a good possibility that once Niani has been properly evaluated, a treatment plan has been implemented, and specialized support services have been arranged, she will be able to continue to participate in Shana's classroom.

> **?** What is your reaction to these teachers' decision that the families must get help if the children are to remain in their current programs? What differences do you see between the two cases? Do you think each decision was justified?

Policy Implications

Situations like the ones involving Parker and Niani would be easier to resolve if all programs serving young children—child development centers, large and small family child care homes, and primary classrooms—had clearly spelled-out and widely distributed policies about the conditions under which children will be recommended for evaluation and the situations in which a child will need to be referred to another setting because the program does not have the resources or expertise to meet the child's needs.

Case 3: Suspected Child Abuse

Trina, a 5-year-old in Dylan's class, shows classic signs of abuse: multiple bruises, frequent black eyes, and psychological withdrawal. Her mother, who appears to be easily agitated, says that Trina falls often, but Dylan has not observed any clumsiness while Trina is at school. Dylan is well aware that, by law, teachers must report suspicions of abuse to their local child protective services agency.

> **What is your first reaction to this case? To whom does Dylan have obligations? What should he consider to help him decide how to act?**

It can be challenging to calmly and competently take the necessary steps to address situations in which you suspect child abuse or neglect. However, it is important to remember that when you suspect child maltreatment, you are required to follow the law's requirements to report your suspicion to the appropriate authorities while you ensure children's safety, take steps to understand families' circumstances and sustain positive relationships with them, and access community resources that protect children and support families.

Advance training and open, honest staff discussions of situations that involve suspected abuse will help you sort through the issues, address strong feelings, and make some of the most difficult decisions that you will face in working with young children.

Our deliberations about suspected child abuse are always grounded in Principle 1.1 in the Code:

> P-1.1—Above all, we shall not harm children. We shall not participate in practices that are emotionally damaging, physically harmful, disrespectful, degrading, dangerous, exploitative, or intimidating to children. **This principle has precedence over all others in this Code**.

Determine the Nature of the Problem

This situation clearly involves ethics, as it involves issues of right and wrong, duties and obligations. But it is *not* an ethical dilemma; it involves an ethical and legal responsibility. Once Dylan observes evidence that Trina may have suffered physical harm, he must meet his ethical and legal responsibility to report what he has seen.

1. Identify the Conflicting Responsibilities

Dylan's primary responsibility is to the child. He must also be respectful of the family, but in this situation it is secondary to his obligation to ensure the child's safety. Because he has seen the bruises, black eyes, and evidence of Trina's psychological stress, he realizes that he has no alternative but to report the suspected abuse.

2. Brainstorm Possible Resolutions

If there were only suspicious signs but no visible indication of physical abuse, Dylan could consider talking with the mother about his concerns and reminding her that as a mandated reporter he must report her to child protective services if he sees signs of abuse. Once he observes the signs, however, brainstorming resolutions is not possible.

3. Consider Ethical Finesse

Dylan cannot finesse this situation—he has to act.

 Have you worked with a child whom you suspected was abused or neglected? What did you do? What resources did you use to help you address the issue?

4. Look for Guidance in the NAEYC Code

The early childhood educator's responsibilities in this case are spelled out clearly in the Code. These Ideals and Principles in the Ethical Responsibilities to Children section are applicable in this situation:

> I-1.4—To appreciate the vulnerability of children and their dependence on adults.

> P-1.1—Above all, we shall not harm children. We shall not participate in practices that are emotionally damaging, physically harmful, disrespectful, degrading, dangerous, exploitative, or intimidating to children. **This principle has precedence over all others in this Code**.

The following two Principles apply specifically to situations that involve suspected child abuse:

> P-1.8—We shall be familiar with the risk factors for and symptoms of child abuse and neglect, including physical, sexual, verbal, and emotional abuse and physical,

emotional, educational, and medical neglect. We shall know and follow state laws and community procedures that protect children against abuse and neglect.

P-1.9—When we have reasonable cause to suspect child abuse or neglect, we shall report it to the appropriate community agency and follow up to ensure that appropriate action has been taken. When appropriate, parents or guardians will be informed that the referral will be or has been made.

Dylan should also note that Ideal 2.2 relating to families is relevant to this situation and reminds him to make every effort to maintain his relationship with the mother:

I-2.2—To develop relationships of mutual trust and create partnerships with the families we serve.

5. Decide on a Justifiable Course of Action

Dylan has been carefully documenting his observations of Trina's pattern of withdrawn behavior and the signs of physical abuse. He discusses the situation with Charlene, the program director. They are both well aware that the law and the NAEYC Code explicitly mandate that Dylan file a report with the child protective services agency because he has reasonable cause (has seen visible signs) to suspect that abuse has occurred. With Charlene's complete support, Dylan reports the situation to the child protection agency.

Dylan knows that it is not his responsibility to collect irrefutable evidence that Trina has been harmed—that is the job of child protective services personnel. If they conclude that intervention is needed, the appropriate state agency will take action to protect the child and assist the family.

But Charlene and Dylan both know the center's obligation doesn't end with making the report. Dylan has developed a trusting relationship with Trina's grandmother, who often cares for her after school. He follows up his report to child protective services by contacting her to talk about possible strategies to ensure Trina's safety and to support the family in seeking counseling.

And finally, Dylan and Charlene will check on the disposition of the case in the child protective services agency, continue to provide nurturing support to the child as long as she is in the center, and work at keeping channels of communication open with the family.

> **?** What thoughts and feelings do you imagine the teacher and director had when they realized they must report their suspicions of child abuse? What kind of community resources would be helpful for the family?

Think About this Ethical Responsibility

The Code directs you to "be familiar with the risk factors for and symptoms of child abuse and neglect." This information is included in many early childhood textbooks and other professional publications. In addition, laws in most states require that teachers receive training on recognizing and reporting suspected child abuse and neglect. These laws determine the length and content of the required trainings. Child care regulations typically require programs to document that all employees are in compliance with these mandates.

If you work in a school or child care center, you are likely to be offered training through your workplace. Your employer may also share publications and websites that offer information for teachers on preventing child abuse and neglect. If this training is not offered, do some reading on your own or take a workshop that addresses risk factors and reporting procedures. You can find resources on the Prevent Child Abuse America and Mayo Clinic websites and through your state's child protective services agency.

Learning about abuse and neglect and reporting procedures is the first step in preparing yourself to protect the children in your care. Another important step is to find ways, whenever possible, to prevent child maltreatment before it occurs. Be alert to interactions between adult family members and children that suggest a child is at risk of being mistreated; be aware of changes in children's behavior; recognize signs that a family is facing extraordinary stress; or notice when a child's basic needs are not being met. When you notice these warning signs, offer support by expressing your concern and asking if you or your director can help. In the Suspected Child Abuse case, Dylan might wonder if he could have done more to protect the child and her family by, for example, noticing how stressed Trina's mother was and offering assistance. Steps to prevent child abuse are most likely to be successful if you have a trusting relationship with the family before it is necessary to express your concerns.

When you see signs that make you suspect physical abuse or neglect, carefully document your observations. Describe any injuries and their location. Take pictures of a child's injuries if doing so will not upset him (CDSS 2011). You might ask another teacher to observe as well, to make sure you both see the same thing and interpret it the same way. It is important to be as accurate and objective as possible and to be confident that there is cause for concern before you make a report. A false report can do a great deal of harm. One of the authors of this book experienced a situation in which a teacher reported a family to child protective services after repeatedly noticing what appeared to be bruises on a young child's buttocks. The child protective services investigation showed that what the teacher had seen were in fact birthmarks and not evidence of abuse. It would have been better for the teacher to ask a family member about the marks before jumping to a conclusion that proved to be false and created a great deal of stress for the family.

When you suspect child abuse or neglect, it may be helpful to contact the child protective services agency for advice before you decide whether you need to file a report. They can tell you signs to look for and questions to ask, or not ask, the child.

As a mandated reporter, you shoulder very important responsibilities. There are serious consequences for mistakes. Be informed so that you can fulfill your obligations and protect the children in your care.

Cultural Issues Related to Child Abuse

Significant cultural differences exist in families' childrearing practices, particularly with regard to appropriate forms of discipline. While corporal punishment is not prohibited by law in the United States, severe punishment that causes physical harm to a child can cross the line and become child abuse.

Situations that involve cultural differences in childrearing and appropriate discipline can be particularly challenging for teachers. An example is the case of a first grade teacher who worked hard to understand and embrace the culture of the families in her class and had a very good working relationship with the father of an apparently well-adjusted boy. After the father mentioned that he regularly hit his child with a belt to teach him how to behave, the teacher noticed signs of welts on the child's back and legs that could have been left by a belt and its buckle.

The teacher realized that cultural differences about appropriate discipline for young children were likely at the core of this situation and that the father's assumptions about appropriate childrearing were probably very different from community norms expressed in child abuse laws. This situation was difficult because the teacher typically sought to honor the childrearing practices of the families of children in her class. Yet even when cultural differences and a good relationship with a family member are present, a teacher has the same legal and moral obligation to report abuse as she does in every other situation in which abuse is suspected. Gonzalez-Mena (2008), in addressing the difficult issues involved in assessing child abuse in cross-cultural situations, offers the following advice:

> You're bound by law to report suspected physical abuse (physical punishment that leaves marks on the child). Be sure parents know this from the start so they won't feel betrayed if you have to report suspected abuse. ... Be respectful of their differing beliefs, but clear about the law. (139)

In this situation the teacher met with the father to explain that the child protection laws in their community did not permit harsh corporal punishment, usually defined as leaving a mark. She told him that she was required by law and by professional ethical guidelines to report evidence of child abuse. She hoped that the child protective services worker who would handle the case would work with this father to improve his parenting skills.

Policy Implications

Programs can minimize misunderstandings about corporal punishment when they develop clear policies about child abuse and let families know that programs have an obligation to watch for and report suspected child abuse. These policies should be in writing and given to families when they enroll their child in the program. The information should be distributed to all families and translated into families' home languages if necessary. This information may help families better understand community definitions of abuse and neglect and teachers' obligations when they see evidence of child maltreatment. Had these practices been implemented in the situation above, a referral to a child protective services agency may not have been necessary. Some programs (and some states) require families to sign a statement that they are aware that teachers are, by law, mandated to report suspected child abuse or neglect.

Reflection on Ethical Situations that Involve Children

The first two scenarios presented in this chapter demonstrate how early childhood educators can systematically approach situations that require them to balance the needs of an individual child with those of a group. Other similar situations may arise. A parent may ask that a teacher always escort his child to the bathroom even though the bathroom is visible from the classroom and is just a short distance away. A family might want their child to be supervised in the classroom in cold, wet weather instead of going outdoors, even though all staff members need to be outside to provide adequate supervision. These types of cases, which require a teacher to balance his responsibilities to a child with those he has to the child's family, will be discussed in Chapter 5.

The third scenario illustrates how to approach a well-founded suspicion of child abuse. Together, these cases emphasize the seriousness of early childhood educators' commitment to the safety and well-being of all children and describe strategies they can use to ensure that these responsibilities are always a priority.

Early Childhood Educators Can Help Prevent Child Abuse and Neglect

Early childhood educators are often the first professionals besides health care providers to interact with young children and their families. They can be a first line of defense against abuse and neglect. Consider these strategies:

- Be aware of the indicators of child abuse and neglect.

- Inform families that you have an obligation to watch for and report signs that indicate possible physical, sexual, or emotional abuse and neglect. Include this information in your program's orientation and in the school's handbook.

- Build strong relationships with families before problems occur so that you have developed a foundation of mutual trust and respect if suspicions arise.

- Offer workshops to help family members learn positive ways of relating to and guiding their children, and inform them about community resources on positive guidance.

- Use resources such as your local child protective service agency and the NAEYC Code of Ethical Conduct to help you know what to do when you suspect abuse or neglect.

- Let children know that it is never okay for someone to hurt them and that they can share concerns and feelings with trusted adults.

5

Ethical Responsibilities to Families

Families are of primary importance in children's development. Because the family and the early childhood practitioner have a common interest in the child's well-being, we acknowledge a primary responsibility to bring about communication, cooperation, and collaboration between the home and early childhood program in ways that enhance the child's development.

—NAEYC Code of Ethical Conduct

Section II of the NAEYC Code of Ethical Conduct, Ethical Responsibilities to Families, acknowledges that while your primary responsibility is to the welfare and education of young children, you also have important responsibilities to children's families. To work effectively with all families, early childhood educators appreciate the role culture plays in the ways families care for their children and how it influences families' expectations and dreams for their children's future. The 2011 reaffirmation and update of the Code highlights the importance of ensuring cultural consistency between children's homes and their education programs. The importance of honoring families' cultures and childrearing practices is the focus of some of the Ideals and Principles in this section of the Code.

Ideals

Nine Ideals in the Code specifically address responsibilities to families (see page 130 in Appendix B). They address such topics as building trusting partnerships with families, respecting each family's culture and preferences, and enhancing families' understanding of their children's development.

The guidance provided by the second section of the administrator supplement, which addresses ethical responsibilities to families, is particularly important for administrators because they frequently encounter ethical issues as they work with the families of the children they serve. This section's Ideals emphasize the importance of forging strong, respectful partnerships with all families and supporting families' efforts to advocate on their children's behalf (see page 138 in Appendix C).

Principles

This section of the Code includes 15 Principles (or rules of professional conduct) that identify your responsibilities to families (see pages 130–131 in Appendix B). These Principles highlight the importance of communicating with families, involving them in their children's education, and maintaining confidentiality.

The administrator supplement contains 11 Principles addressing topics such as communicating with families in accessible ways, applying policies fairly to families, and endeavoring to support both staff and families in disagreements (see pages 138–139 in Appendix B).

Typical Ethical Issues Involving Families

Some of the ethical issues you will face involve addressing a family member's request that you do something you do not believe is in the child's best interests or that you do not have the resources or expertise to implement. Other issues arise when families are embroiled in contentious divorce or custody disputes, when you are asked to share confidential information, or when you suspect child abuse or neglect.

While most professionals serve and have allegiance to just one client, pediatricians and early childhood educators—both of whom provide services to children as well as to children's adult family members—are notable exceptions. We refer to situations in which professionals must balance their obligations to a child with those they have to the child's family as **complex-client cases.**

This chapter describes five complex-client scenarios. In each one, an early childhood educator has conflicting obligations to a child and that child's family.

Case 4: The Nap

Kali, the mother of 4-year-old Chase, has asked his teacher, Sondra, to keep him from napping in the afternoon. She tells Sondra, "Whenever Chase naps during the day, he stays up until past 10:00 at night. I have to get up at 5:00 in the morning to go to work, and I am not getting enough sleep." Along with all the other children, Chase takes a one-hour nap almost every day. Sondra feels that he needs it to engage in activities and stay in good spirits through the afternoon.

Honoring Different Cultural Perspectives

An important goal for all early childhood educators is to create an environment that values and supports all families. As communities become more diverse, it is vital that you develop **cultural competence**—the knowledge and skills needed to work effectively with children and families whose cultural backgrounds and experiences are different from your own (Harper Browne, Castro, & Lucier 2016).

Cultural competence begins with self-awareness. What cultural biases do you bring to your work with young children? How do your biases impact your interactions with children and your expectations for them? Understanding how culture impacts you as well as the children and families you work with can help you discover how to honor differing values, beliefs, and childrearing practices as you support children's development.

Teachers from Western cultures may view aspects of childrearing very differently from those from other cultural backgrounds. Gonzalez-Mena (2008) and Harper Browne, Castro, and Lucier (2016) describe some of the ways that differences in culturally determined values can cause misunderstandings between early childhood educators and children's families. There may be cultural differences in the way families view

- **Personal possessions:** What possessions are children expected to share, and which are for their use only?

- **Cooperation and competition:** Are children given many opportunities to cooperate to be successful, or are they expected to compete with one another for recognition?

- **The development of independence:** Are young children expected to feed themselves and go to sleep on their own, or do adults support interdependence by helping children with these tasks?

- **The way children's behavior should be controlled:** Is it considered important for children to develop self-control, or do families require strict obedience and punish children to enforce parental expectations?

An important component of achieving cultural competence is the ability to read individuals' body language. That means taking care to observe how individuals from cultures different from your own use personal space and under what circumstances they smile, touch, and make eye contact with each other. It may also be helpful to realize that cultural groups have different ways of defining what it means to be on time. These and other practices tend to vary across cultures—and within them as well—and you may misinterpret well-intentioned actions if you do not take cultural differences into account.

Your success in navigating cultural differences and in achieving cultural competence will require you to form partnerships with families. The goal of working together to support children's development and learning can be especially challenging when teachers and families bring different cultural styles, worldviews, values, and traditions to their relationships.

Seek information, guidance, and tools from individuals and programs to develop and evaluate your cultural competence. Organizations such as NAEYC and Zero to Three are helpful, as are publications such as *Anti-Bias Education for Young Children and Ourselves* (Derman-Sparks & Edwards 2010).

Developing cultural competence reflects a respect for the rich mosaic of cultures that make up the United States. Cultural beliefs and values permeate every interaction between children and adults and between the adults who work with young children. It is your responsibility as an early childhood educator to learn about the cultures, traditions, worldviews, and values of the families and communities you serve so that your work with children will help prepare them for success in their home communities and beyond.

Do you work with families whose values, beliefs, or childrearing practices are different from your own? Have cultural differences created special challenges for you? How have you dealt with the issues you've encountered?

What is your first reaction to this situation? To whom does Sondra have obligations? What factors should she consider when responding to this request?

1. Identify the Conflicting Responsibilities

2. Brainstorm Possible Resolutions

3. Consider Ethical Finesse

> **?** Have you ever had to choose between a parent's and a child's needs? What did you do in that situation? What resources did you use to resolve the issue?

4. Look for Guidance in the NAEYC Code

- Respect the dignity, worth, and uniqueness of each individual (child, family member, and colleague)
- Recognize that children and adults achieve their full potential in the context of relationships that are based on trust and respect

Next, she turns to the Ideals in the sections of the Code on Ethical Responsibilities to Children and Ethical Responsibilities to Families. She notes that the following Ideals are relevant:

I-1.4—To appreciate the vulnerability of children and their dependence on adults.

I-1.5—To create and maintain safe and healthy settings that foster children's social, emotional, cognitive, and physical development and that respect their dignity and their contributions.

I-2.4—To listen to families, acknowledge and build upon their strengths and competencies, and learn from families as we support them in their task of nurturing children.

I-2.6—To acknowledge families' childrearing values and their right to make decisions for their children.

I-2.8—To help family members enhance their understanding of their children, as staff are enhancing their understanding of each child through communications with families, and support family members in the continuing development of their skills as parents.

These Ideals confirm that Sondra has important responsibilities to Chase's well-being and also to his family's needs and values. She wants to honor Kali's wishes, but she is convinced that Chase needs the opportunity to sleep at least an hour each day if he is going to have a good afternoon.

She then considers the Code's Principles about teachers' actions related to children and families, with special attention to P-1.1.

P-1.1—Above all, we shall not harm children. We shall not participate in practices that are emotionally damaging, physically harmful, disrespectful, degrading, dangerous, exploitative, or intimidating to children. **This principle has precedence over all others in this Code**.

She notes these other relevant Principles:

P-2.2—We shall inform families of program philosophy, policies, curriculum, assessment system, cultural practices, and personnel qualifications, and explain why we teach as we do—which should be in accordance with our ethical responsibilities to children.

P-2.4—We shall ensure that the family is involved in significant decisions affecting their child.

5. Decide on a Justifiable Course of Action

When her efforts to modify the nap routine don't resolve the issue, Sondra is more convinced than ever that Chase's emotional and physical well-being are dependent on his afternoon nap. She now faces a difficult predicament. Based on her review of the Code and her best professional judgment, she realizes she must give first priority to Chase's needs and that she has to gently and respectfully tell Kali that she cannot deprive Chase of his afternoon nap.

This situation has made Sondra appreciate the kind of backing the NAEYC Code provides. The Code added the wisdom of the profession to her carefully considered decision. It did not make this unpopular position any easier, but she feels confident knowing that she systematically weighed her conflicting responsibilities and that she is not alone when she stands firm in doing what she is convinced is right for the child. We often say, "When your back is against the wall, the Code of Ethical Conduct can sometimes hold up the wall."

When Sondra meets with Kali, she explains that she has tried several changes to Chase's naptime routine and realizes that keeping him from sleeping would be harmful—he needs a nap to function in the afternoon. Sondra shares with Kali the NAEYC Code and in particular the Principle that directs her not to participate in practices that are harmful to children.

Sondra asks Kali to respect her decision and urges her not to let it impair their positive working relationship. She also expresses her hope that they can continue to work together to support Chase's growth and development. In addition, she reminds Kali that children grow and mature quickly and that she will watch for signs that indicate Chase no longer needs an afternoon nap. For now, however, she says she must insist that the naptime routine remain unchanged.

Sondra realizes there may be negative consequences to this decision. Kali might decide to withdraw Chase from the program and place him in another preschool that may be more responsive to her requests. Depending on the supply and demand for child care in their community, the program director may put pressure on Sondra to do whatever is necessary to honor Kali's request. Teachers presented with this kind of ultimatum sometimes face the additional dilemma of whether to stand firm in their decision or to conform to the demands of an administration with different priorities.

> **?** **Do you believe Sondra's decision to deny Chase's mother's request can be justified by relying on the Code? What would you have done?**

Case 5: Messy Play

Reena is the mother of 3-year-old Mia, a child in Alicia's class. Reena has asked Alicia to keep her daughter clean and not allow her to participate in art or sensory activities that are messy or dirty. Mia cries at bath time when her mother has to wash paint from under her nails and from her arms, legs, and hair, and this distresses them both. It is also important to Reena that Mia look neat and clean for school, and Reena has had to replace many of her daughter's school clothes because they are stained from messy play activities. Reena spends a lot of time and effort to keep Mia and her clothes clean, which makes it difficult to attend to her other obligations in the evening.

 What is your first reaction to this situation? To whom does Alicia have obligations? What factors should she consider when deciding what to do?

1. Identify the Conflicting Responsibilities

2. Brainstorm Possible Resolutions

> **?** Has a member of a child's family ever asked you to modify classroom activities that you believed to be beneficial? Under what circumstances might you be willing to exclude one child from a classroom activity at the family's request?

3. Consider Ethical Finesse

while continuing to allow Mia to participate in messy activities. The school could provide big shirts or smocks as well as shower caps or ribbons to keep long hair out of the way. Alicia could apply a shielding lotion that prevents Mia's hands from getting stained. Reena could send clean clothes from home and the staff could help Mia get washed and changed into them before she leaves in the afternoon or, if the school has a washing machine, the staff could wash Mia's clothes at school so Reena wouldn't have to do that in the evening.

It would also be possible to use finesse in this situation by modifying some classroom practices. Alicia could use only easy-to-clean art materials such as washable paint and markers, and playdough instead of clay; she could show the children how to avoid getting dirty by controlling the art materials; or she could have children use water for painting sidewalks or fences—an activity that looks messy but actually involves no cleanup at all. She could also modify her schedule by planning messy activities for early in the day, giving Mia plenty of time to get clean afterward or by providing longer transitions between activities so there is more time for thorough cleanup. Alicia could schedule a regular once-a-week "messy day" and suggest that families send in clothes the children can change into for messy play.

While Alicia is hopeful that ethical finesse will resolve this issue, she knows it is always a good idea to think about how to proceed if finesse does not work.

4. Look for Guidance in the NAEYC Code

When her attempts to use ethical finesse do not resolve the dilemma, Alicia turns first to the NAEYC Code of Ethical Conduct's Core Values for guidance. She finds that three items are relevant to the situation:

- Base our work on knowledge of how children develop and learn
- Respect the dignity, worth, and uniqueness of each individual (child, family member, and colleague)
- Recognize that children and adults achieve their full potential in the context of relationships that are based on trust and respect

Alicia particularly appreciates the field's strong historical commitment to all areas of children's development and its equally strong commitment to work closely with families and to respect their values and childrearing practices. Alicia must determine whether it is more important to prioritize strengthening her relationship with this mother or to meet the developmental needs of this child.

The first option, to let Mia continue to participate in messy activities, could be supported by a number of items in the Code that assert that the child's well-being is of primary concern and that under no circumstances should a child be harmed. As in all ethical situations that involve children, Alicia must first consider P-1.1:

> Above all, we shall not harm children. We shall not participate in practices that are emotionally damaging, physically harmful, disrespectful, degrading, dangerous,

exploitative, or intimidating to children. **This principle has precedence over all others in this Code**.

Other ethical responsibilities to children reflected in the Code's Ideals could support the decision to let Mia continue to participate in activities that are likely to be messy:

I-1.2—To base program practices upon current knowledge and research in the field of early childhood education, child development, and related disciplines, as well as on particular knowledge of each child.

I-1.5—To create and maintain safe and healthy settings that foster children's social, emotional, cognitive, and physical development and that respect their dignity and their contributions.

If, after careful observation and reflection, Alicia determines that it would be detrimental to Mia if she were not allowed to participate in messy sensory activities, she would be justified in declining Mia's mother's request. She could explain that excluding Mia from sensory activities would deprive her of meaningful hands-on learning experiences and that she would miss out on significant peer interactions. In addition, not allowing access to these activities could be harmful if Mia had issues with sensory integration and required activities that addressed her needs.

The second possible course of action, to do what Reena asks and prevent Mia from participating in messy activities, can be justified by reviewing the items in the Code that highlight the importance of respect for and collaboration with families. These include

I-2.2—To develop relationships of mutual trust and create partnerships with the families we serve.

I-2.5—To respect the dignity and preferences of each family.

I-2.6—To acknowledge families' childrearing values and their right to make decisions for their children.

P-2.6—As families share information with us about their children and families, we shall ensure that families' input is an important contribution to the planning and implementation of the program.

5. Decide on a Justifiable Course of Action

Since a strong case can be made for either alternative and both can be justified by relying on the Code, Alicia needs to weigh the costs and benefits of the choices. If Alicia is confident that Mia would not be seriously harmed by not having access to messy play, she would be justified in complying with Reena's request. This decision would help build trust with Reena and enhance their collaborative relationship. If Alicia decides on this course of action, she could continue to help Reena understand the benefits of sensory experiences to children's development. Alicia might also share some ways other families handle evening cleanup. If Alicia does limit Mia's access to the messy activities available to other children, she must do

Do you think Alicia's decision is justifiable? What would you have done in this situation?

Case 6: Don't Let My Son Dress Up as a Girl!

Four-year-old Victor enjoys playing dress-up in the dramatic play area. Typically a quiet and reserved child, he becomes a leader when playing dress-up, particularly when he is pretending to be a firefighter, princess, bumblebee, or mom. One day his father, Leo, who rarely visits the center, comes to pick up his son and sees Victor dressed in a pink princess costume. Leo is visibly annoyed and tells Meredith, Victor's teacher, that he does not want her to allow Victor to play in the dress-up area in the future. He then orders Victor to change and quickly leaves with him.

The center is devoted to fostering relationships with all of its families, and Meredith has recently made great strides in attracting Victor's family to potlucks and school workdays. The staff collectively believe that in addition to building children's imaginations, dramatic play enhances their social and communication skills and is an integral part of the learning process that gives children opportunities to develop abstract thinking, literacy, math, and social studies skills.

What is your first reaction to this case? To whom does Meredith have obligations? What should she consider when making a decision?

1. Identify the Conflicting Responsibilities

2. Brainstorm Possible Resolutions

choose what and how he plays while Meredith works with his father to help him appreciate the benefits of pretend play.

3. Consider Ethical Finesse

This case is a particularly good candidate for ethical finesse. Meredith is hopeful that by sharing her professional knowledge about child development and the benefits of dramatic play with Victor's father, he may begin to think differently about the situation. She thinks it might help to invite Leo to spend time in the classroom to see for himself that Victor enjoys a variety of activities, and that when he does dress up he tries a number of different roles besides princess. She could also use the school's monthly newsletter to highlight the importance of dramatic play.

Another way Meredith might finesse this issue is by making changes to the dress-up center by offering more gender-neutral choices—such as scarves and pieces of colorful fabric—to inspire non-gender-specific play.

4. Look for Guidance in the NAEYC Code

Meredith turns to the Code's Core Values, Ideals, and Principles for guidance on her responsibilities to children and the importance of nurturing positive relationships with families.

The following Core Values are particularly applicable to Meredith's situation:

- Base our work on knowledge of how children develop and learn
- Appreciate and support the bond between the child and family
- Respect diversity in children, families, and colleagues

These Ideals also help guide her thinking:

> I-1.2—To base program practices upon current knowledge and research in the field of early childhood education, child development, and related disciplines, as well as on particular knowledge of each child.

> I-1.3—To recognize and respect the unique qualities, abilities, and potential of each child.

> I-1.5—To create and maintain safe and healthy settings that foster children's social, emotional, cognitive, and physical development and that respect their dignity and their contributions.

> I-2.2—To develop relationships of mutual trust and create partnerships with the families we serve.

> I-2.5—To respect the dignity and preferences of each family and to make an effort to learn about its structure, culture, language, customs, and beliefs.

I-2.6—To acknowledge families' childrearing values and their right to make decisions for their children.

I-2.8—To help family members enhance their understanding of their children … and support the continuing development of their skills as parents.

Meredith locates the following applicable Principles:

P-1.1—Above all, we shall not harm children. We shall not participate in practices that are emotionally damaging, physically harmful, disrespectful, degrading, dangerous, exploitative, or intimidating to children. **This principle has precedence over all others in this Code**.

P-1.2—We shall care for and educate children in positive emotional and social environments that are cognitively stimulating and that support each child's culture, language, ethnicity, and family structure.

P-2.2—We shall inform families of program philosophy, policies, curriculum, assessment system, and personnel qualifications, and explain why we teach as we do—which should be in accordance with our ethical responsibilities to children.

P-2.4—We shall ensure that the family is involved in significant decisions affecting their child.

P-2.5—We shall make every effort to communicate effectively with all families in a language that they understand. We shall use community resources for translation and interpretation when we do not have sufficient resources in our own programs.

5. Decide on a Justifiable Course of Action

Meredith decides that the best resolution to this dilemma would be to use ethical finesse to help Victor's father appreciate the value of dramatic play and to assure him that this kind of play is not unusual or cause for concern.

If finesse is not effective, Meredith realizes she should involve her director—and perhaps the other teachers in the center—in helping her make a decision. If together they determine that restricting Victor's activities in the dramatic play area would cause harm both to him and to his classmates and therefore they should refuse to honor Leo's instruction, their decision would be guided by Principle 1.1: "Above all, we shall not harm children."

If this is seen as the most justifiable course of action, it will be essential that Meredith meet with Victor's parents to discuss her decision to continue to allow Victor to dress up and act out his desired roles. Meredith will need to be prepared to accept negative reactions to this decision.

> **?** Do you believe Meredith would be justified in refusing to honor the father's request if her attempts to finesse this dilemma are not effective? What would you say to a family member who made a similar request?

Four-year-old Michael's mother is volunteering in her son's classroom and observes him playing in a ballerina skirt and sparkly shoes. She firmly instructs Michael to take them off and to put on the firefighter's hat and boots, to try on the cowboy hat, or to do "something that boys do." Michael complies but soon leaves the dramatic play area.

Later, his mother tells Ana, Michael's teacher, that Michael consistently plays female roles at home and shows little interest in toys and activities typically associated with boys. This frustrates and angers Michael's father, and he has instructed the mother to not allow Michael to play with "girl stuff," even at school. "I don't know what to do," the mother tells Ana with a sigh. "I just want Michael to be happy."

Case 7: Reporting Classroom Behavior

Four-year-old Mateo's aggressive behavior has become a challenge. He has kicked and injured a classmate on the playground, and other incidents have become more frequent. His teacher, Alexis, has discussed the problem with his parents and has been developing a plan to help him control his emotions and behavior. Alexis is glad when Mateo's mother, Nadia, stops by the classroom to talk one day, but Alexis doesn't know how to respond when Nadia tells Alexis how important it is to her and her husband that Mateo behave in school and insists that the teacher report to her immediately if Mateo misbehaves so they can punish him at home. Alexis is concerned because, based on her observations of Mateo's interactions with his parents, she believes the family uses a harsh approach to discipline.

> **?** What is your first reaction to this case? To whom does Alexis have responsibilities? What should she consider before responding to this request?

the comments and feedback from many experienced teachers of young children that were reported in the column.

Determine the Nature of the Problem

This situation involves ethics because Alexis must decide how to balance her competing professional obligations. Should she comply with Nadia's request to inform her whenever Mateo behaves aggressively toward his classmates, or should she refuse to routinely notify his parents—which might prevent Mateo from being harshly disciplined at home? This is an ethical dilemma because there is more than one justifiable response. Alexis knows she must keep in the forefront her responsibility to protect both Mateo and his classmates from harm, even as she seeks to honor her obligations to Mateo's parents, who have a right to be informed about their child's behavior. She recognizes that she also has responsibilities to the other children's families, who have reason to be concerned when Mateo's behavior puts their children's safety at risk.

1. Identify the Conflicting Responsibilities

The crux of this the issue lies in balancing Mateo's need for protection from harm with his family's request that they be informed about any aggression he shows during the school day so that they can discipline him at home.

Alexis is mindful of her responsibility to keep Mateo and his classmates safe and to foster their social and emotional development in a nurturing environment. She recognizes that she has the competing responsibility to keep Mateo's family informed about his experiences in school and to respect their childrearing values and their right to make decisions affecting their child.

Upon reflection, she realizes she also has responsibilities to her coteacher and other teachers at this center. Complying with this request could lead other families to expect frequent and detailed reports about their children's school-day experiences. This practice would be time consuming and could divert the teachers' attention from their other responsibilities.

2. Brainstorm Possible Resolutions

Alexis could decide that her primary responsibility is to respect the family's childrearing values and their right to make decisions concerning their child. For that reason, Alexis could honor Nadia's request by regularly informing her about Mateo's behavior and letting the parents decide how to handle the situation at home (assuming that their discipline does not become abusive). This decision prioritizes the importance of maintaining a positive and collaborative relationship with Mateo's family.

The other justifiable resolution would be for Alexis to decide that her primary responsibility is to Mateo. If she chose this alternative, she would not tell Mateo's mother every time he harmed other children because she wants to protect him from potentially harsh discipline.

She would need to have a frank but respectful conversation with Nadia in hopes that she would maintain her good relationship with the family.

> **?** Have you ever been in a situation when you believed complying with a family member's request could put a child's safety at risk? What did you do? What resources helped you handle that dilemma?

3. Consider Ethical Finesse

This dilemma is particularly difficult because it requires Alexis to choose between two undesirable alternatives. She runs the risk of damaging her relationship with the family if she decides not to report Mateo's behavior, and if she does report each incident, she believes there is a good chance he will be severely punished.

For these reasons, she concludes that the best alternative would be to find an effective way to finesse this dilemma. Alexis could begin this process by gathering more information about Mateo and his family. She could ask if his parents have observed aggressive behavior at home and if so, how they handle it. She could go on to ask whether there might be a health issue (e.g., a hearing problem or allergies) that could be related to the aggressive behavior, if he is sleeping and eating well, or if there is any unusual stress at home. She can ask Nadia if she thinks any of these factors could be causing Mateo's challenging behaviors.

She might also examine her own practice and work with her director or a specialist to determine when and why Mateo becomes aggressive. Is he most likely to have difficulty during transitions, or perhaps at the end of the day when he is tired and hungry? Could the classroom's daily schedule or room arrangement be contributing to his behavior? Is he overwhelmed by expectations? Does he need more novelty and stimulation? Are other children provoking him? Might he be more successful in another classroom? Alexis hopes that by identifying circumstances that trigger Mateo's aggression, it can be prevented.

It would also be advisable for Alexis to meet with Mateo's family to discuss positive discipline techniques and to demonstrate strategies for effectively guiding his behavior. She could suggest that together they develop a guidance plan with clear expectations and consequences that would apply both at home and at school, and then meet regularly to compare notes about how this approach is going. During this process Alexis could ensure that the lines of communication remain open by agreeing to call Nadia every day. She would, however, use these calls mainly to report Mateo's positive interactions and would manage any problems in the classroom when they happen. In this way she would be honoring Nadia's request for frequent reports about Mateo's day while strengthening their relationship by communicating regularly.

4. Look for Guidance in the NAEYC Code

If none of her attempts to finesse this issue succeeds in reducing Mateo's aggressive behavior, Alexis needs to rely on the Code to support the difficult decision she must make. A number of Core Values, Ideals, and Principles addressing her responsibilities to children as well as the importance of creating nurturing relationships with all families relate to this dilemma.

She identifies the following Core Values as relevant to this situation:

- Base our work on knowledge of how children develop and learn
- Appreciate and support the bond between the child and family
- Respect the dignity, worth, and uniqueness of each individual (child, family member, and colleague)
- Recognize that children and adults achieve their full potential in the context of relationships that are based on trust and respect

Alexis studies these Ideals and Principles in the Code that relate to her ethical responsibilities to children:

> I-1.2—To base program practices upon current knowledge and research in the field of early childhood education, child development, and related disciplines, as well as on particular knowledge of each child.

> I-1.4—To appreciate the vulnerability of children and their dependence on adults.

> I-1.5—To create and maintain safe and healthy settings that foster children's social, emotional, cognitive, and physical development and that respect their dignity and their contributions.

> P-1.1—Above all, we shall not harm children. We shall not participate in practices that are emotionally damaging, physically harmful, disrespectful, degrading, dangerous, exploitative, or intimidating to children. **This principle has precedence over all others in this Code**.

Next she looks at Ideals related to her responsibilities to families:

> I-2.2—To develop relationships of mutual trust and create partnerships with the families we serve.

> I-2.4—To listen to families, acknowledge and build upon their strengths and competencies, and learn from families as we support them in their task of nurturing children.

> I-2.6—To acknowledge families' childrearing values and their right to make decisions for their children.

> I-2.7—To share information about each child's education and development with families and to help them understand and appreciate the current knowledge base of the early childhood profession.

I-2.8—To help family members enhance their understanding of their children, as staff are enhancing their understanding of each child through communications with families, and support family members in the continuing development of their skills as parents.

5. Decide on a Justifiable Course of Action

When efforts at finesse are not successful and Mateo's aggressive behavior persists, Alexis decides she will refuse to routinely report Mateo's misbehavior to Nadia. This decision is based on the first principle in the NAEYC Code, which directs early childhood educators to make children's safety and well-being their first priority. That means that even though other items in the Code strongly support maintaining close, collaborative relationships with families and honoring their childrearing values, Alexis is justified in deciding not to inform Mateo's mother every time he is too rough or aggressive at school. A contributing factor that supports this position is that if Mateo knew his teacher was reporting his behavior to his parents, he might become afraid and no longer feel that school is a safe, nurturing place.

Alexis will invite Nadia and her husband to meet with her so she can explain her decision and reiterate how much she wants to maintain their positive working relationship. Alexis may have already shared some ideas about effective guidance techniques while trying to finesse this dilemma. During this follow-up meeting, she'll explain that punishing Mateo at home is not likely to be effective; responding to inappropriate behavior immediately is more effective at helping children understand the effects of their actions and learn to control their behavior. Alexis can review the guidance plan if one was developed previously, and she can make certain the parents understand the techniques being used to address Mateo's behavior while he is at the center.

During this discussion Alexis will also assure Mateo's parents that she is a professional trained to deal with aggressive behavior in children, and since it is a problem only at school, it is appropriate that it be handled there. She will tell them that she will let them know if there is a serious incident, and if there is, she will definitely solicit their help and support. Alexis will also agree to be available to meet with them anytime they have a specific question about her approach to guidance, and she will remind them that if at some point the center isn't working for their family, they are free to choose a setting that might better meet their needs.

She is hopeful that she can work with Mateo to address her concerns about his behavior while partnering with his family to share guidance strategies she knows are appropriate for young children. Her goal is that she and the family will be able to work together to support his healthy growth and development.

> **?** Do you believe Alexis's decision to refuse to honor Mateo's mother's request was justified? What would you say to a family member who made a similar request?

Policy Implications

This scenario provides another example of how having clear policies in place can help avoid a difficult situation. This issue could have been avoided if the family handbook included a statement making it clear that teachers will provide families with an accurate overview of their child's day, but that they will not report negative behavior to children's families on a regular basis unless absolutely essential. This policy would keep the focus on positive reports and would avoid the risk that the child would be punished at home for something that occurred during the school day.

Case 8: Birthday Cake

Olivia is the director of an early childhood program that is committed to serving healthy foods. The center doesn't serve cookies, cakes, or other foods that are high in sugar, fat, or preservatives. The program's family handbook describes these policies. It states clearly that birthday cakes are not allowed. The nutrition policy strongly encourages families to celebrate special events with healthy foods, such as berries, watermelon, sliced fruit, vegetable plates, and vegetable pizza. Another important part of the program's philosophy is to develop close relationships with all the families. Olivia strives to honor families' values and to warmly welcome children and their families each day.

One morning Mrs. Chang, a mother new to the center who has been shy about participating and whose mastery of English is limited, arrives with a large, elaborately decorated cake to celebrate the birthday of her daughter, Mei-Zhen.

> **What is your first reaction to this case? To whom does Olivia have responsibilities? What should she consider as she prepares to respond to this mother?**

Like the other cases in this chapter, this situation requires an early childhood educator to balance responsibilities to a child with those to the child's family. In this instance, it is the program director who is faced with making a difficult decision. The analysis of this case was first published in the Focus on Ethics column in *Young Children* (Feeney & Freeman 2013). It reflects the comments and feedback from teachers, directors, graduate students, and college faculty who responded to this dilemma.

Determine the Nature of the Problem

This situation involves ethics because Olivia must decide on the right and most fair course of action. It is an ethical dilemma because she must decide if she will follow the center policy designed to promote healthy eating and refuse to serve the birthday cake or disregard the policy and serve the cake. If she refuses, Mrs. Chang is likely to be upset at having her well-intentioned offering rebuffed. If Olivia allows the cake to be served, her relationship with this mother may be preserved but the children will consume an undesirable amount of sugar. Olivia is also well aware that if she allows the cake to be served, families who have followed the no-sweets policy are likely to be upset.

1. Identify the Conflicting Responsibilities

Olivia is faced with the challenge of balancing her responsibilities to Mrs. Chang, to Mei-Zhen, and to her own commitment to the health of all the children in the center. She also has responsibilities to abide by the center's policies and to apply those policies consistently in order to respect the families who have followed them. Finally, Olivia has a responsibility to contribute to the center's efforts to develop a close relationship with the family of every child in the school.

2. Brainstorm Possible Resolutions

The best way for the director to proceed is not clear. One way for Olivia to resolve this dilemma would be to give first priority to her responsibility to promote healthy eating, as described in the center's policies. That means she would acknowledge and thank Mrs. Chang for her contribution and respectfully explain that the cake would not be served because Olivia must abide by the program's policy regarding healthy food. Olivia could invite Mrs. Chang to join the class to celebrate Mei-Zhen's birthday and share the center's healthy snack.

The alternative would be to give first priority to nurturing a good relationship with Mrs. Chang. In that case, Olivia would warmly thank her, take the cake to the classroom, and serve it. If she decides to do that, she would make sure to have the center's policies translated into Mrs. Chang's home language and would review them with her carefully at a later date (using a translator, if necessary). Each of these choices has advantages and disadvantages, and both can be justified using the NAEYC Code.

> **?** Have you ever been in a situation when you felt that following a program policy might damage your relationship with a child's family? What did you do? What resources helped you handle the issue?

3. Consider Ethical Finesse

Olivia does not have very much time to figure out how to use finesse to address this situation—she must respond quickly. She must either thank Mrs. Chang and accept the cake or politely refuse it and ask the mother to take it back home. If she decides to accept the cake, she might suggest that Mei-Zhen's teacher serve very small pieces or send pieces of cake home with children so their families could decide whether or not to serve it. Olivia knows that neither of these alternatives is what Mrs. Chang had in mind when she brought the birthday cake. What's more, Olivia knows that asking Mrs. Chang to agree to one of these options would be difficult because of the language barrier between them. Olivia realizes she must decide quickly if she will honor Mrs. Chang's good intentions or strictly enforce the center's no-sweets policy.

4. Decide on a Justifiable Course of Action

While Olivia does not have time to carefully consider the guidance the Code and the administrator supplement might give her, she intends to consult both documents when she gets back to her office. Fortunately, she is well acquainted with their content and has a good deal of practice applying them to situations she has faced before. She feels confident that the Code could justify either serving or declining to serve the birthday cake. After quickly considering the costs and benefits of each position and looking at the hopeful face of the mother standing in front of her holding the beautiful cake, Olivia decides that the best course of action at that moment is to honor her relationship with the mother and serve the cake. She feels that doing this will have a minimal negative impact on the children's well-being and will provide greater long-term benefits to her relationship with the family than strictly adhering to the program's no-sweets policy.

If you were to face this kind of dilemma yourself, your decision would be influenced by the specifics of the situation, such as your relationship with the mother and your sense of whether she had been informed of, and understood, the no-sweets policy when she brought in the cake You might also consider the feelings of the other families.

> Do you believe Olivia did the right thing by deciding to serve the cake? What might she say about it to the other families? What do you think you would do if faced with a similar dilemma?

5. Look for Guidance in the NAEYC Code

When Olivia returns to her office and consults the Code, she is gratified to find ways that it provides justification for serving the cake. For example, she finds these applicable Core Values:

- Appreciate and support the bond between the child and family
- Respect the dignity, worth, and uniqueness of each individual (child, family member, and colleague)
- Respect diversity in children, families, and colleagues
- Recognize that children and adults achieve their full potential in the context of relationships that are based on trust and respect

She also appreciates that this Core Value from the administrator supplement reminds her that as the program's director, she must consider all children's well-being in every decision she makes:

> The well-being of the children in our care is our primary responsibility, above our obligations to other constituencies.

Olivia believes that Mei-Zhen would likely be very disappointed, and perhaps embarrassed, by having her birthday cake sent home, and that to do so would violate P-1.1:

> Above all, we shall not harm children. We shall not participate in practices that are emotionally damaging, physically harmful, disrespectful, degrading … to children.

She also finds these items that address the importance of building partnerships with families and encouraging their participation.

From the Code:

> I-2.2—To develop relationships of mutual trust and create partnerships with the families we serve.

> I-2.3—To welcome all family members and encourage them to participate in the program.

From the administrator supplement:

> I-2.5—To create and maintain a climate of trust and candor that fosters two-way communication.

> P-2.1—We shall work to create a respectful environment for and a working relationship with all families.

Olivia is also well aware that there are items in the Code that would support a decision to not serve the cake.

From the Code:

> I-1.5—To create and maintain safe and healthy settings that foster children's … physical development,

From the supplement:

> P-2.4—We shall establish clear operating policies and make them available to families in advance of their child entering the program.

> P-2.8—We shall apply all policies regarding obligations to families consistently and fairly.

> P-2.10—We shall respond to families' requests to the extent that the requests are congruent with program philosophy, standards of good practice, and the resources of the program.

Policy Implications

Regardless of which of these two defensible courses of action you believe is preferable, this case highlights the fact that in spite of Olivia's good intentions, and whether or not she decided to serve the cake, she had not successfully communicated with all families as the administrator supplement requires her to do:

> P-2.3—We shall make every attempt to use two-way communication to convey information in ways that are accessible by every family served.

> P-2.4—We shall establish clear operating policies and make them available to families in advance of their child entering the program.

This difficult situation could have been avoided if the program's family handbook had been translated and communicated effectively so that all families were fully informed.

One early childhood leader who responded to this case challenged the assumption that an occasional sweet treat could really be harmful to children and questioned the soundness of this policy, asking "What's the world coming to now where a birthday child can't have birthday cake?" She suggested that in this situation the importance of rituals and the needs of children to experience celebrations in combination with respect for family and culture should override strict adherence to center policy. She proposed that the center could change this policy to allow reasonable servings of birthday cake or other sweets *on special occasions* if there are no regulations that food must come from a specified vendor. Her comments remind us that policies *can* be changed if firsthand experiences and thoughtful reflection convince program personnel that a change would be in children's and families' best interests.

Reflection on Complex-Client Cases

During your career you will no doubt encounter complex-client dilemmas such as the ones in this chapter and others like these:

- A 4-year-old's father asks that you make sure she wears her hooded fleece jacket even though she is often hot and sweaty.
- A 2-year-old's family asks you to move her to the 3s classroom, but you don't think she is ready.
- A family requests that their child not participate in the classroom's customary birthday observations (singing "Happy Birthday" and enjoying a special snack).
- A family insists that a male teacher not be permitted to change their toddler's diaper.
- Families ask that you make the program's curriculum more academic because they are concerned about their children's readiness for future school success.

Ethical finesse will often help you reach a satisfactory resolution to dilemmas like these, but it depends on your ability to listen carefully to understand the family's point of view, communicate your own position effectively, and work collaboratively. Successful finesse is likely to require families, teachers, and administrators to compromise and be receptive to change. Consider the child's probable reaction or the consequences he may experience if there is an exception to the rule. Will excluding a child from the classroom's birthday observances mean that he's missing out on being an accepted member of the classroom community, or can the mother's request be honored without interfering with her child's full participation in other classroom traditions? Will the class's primary care assignments be disrupted if the male teacher is not allowed to change this child's diaper?

Lilian Katz weighed in on this type of case the first time it was discussed in *Young Children*. She noted that "when parental preferences require a child to be excepted from standard program procedures and the teacher judges the exception to jeopardize the child's well-being, the teacher must respectfully decline to honor the parents' wishes" (Feeney, Katz, & Kipnis 1987, 18). This decision is reflected in Principle 1.1 of the Code, which states emphatically that "we will not harm children." This item takes precedence in all of our work with young children and their families. Whenever the well-being of a child is in jeopardy, the child's needs must take precedence over family requests.

However, teachers should make accommodations to honor families' requests provided no harm will come to their child or other children from doing so. These situations may also offer opportunities to provide family members with more information about child development as well as recommended best practices that help strengthen relationships and build classroom community.

You may have noticed that in three of the cases in this chapter, the teacher decided that the child's needs should take precedence over those of the parent; in the other two, the teacher concluded that honoring the family member's request was justifiable and offered the best resolution to the dilemma. Sometimes the dilemmas you face will be similar to those in The Nap, Reporting Classroom Behavior, and Don't Let My Son Dress Up as a Girl! cases, in which, after careful analysis and attempts to apply ethical finesse, you decide to politely but firmly deny the family's request. In other instances, such as in the Messy Play and Birthday Cake cases, after determining that doing so would not substantially harm children, it may be appropriate to give precedence to a family's request in an attempt to strengthen your relationship with the family.

Cases such as Don't Let My Son Dress Up as a Girl! may bring to light strongly held, culturally determined family beliefs. They require an extra measure of respect for a family's culture, along with flexibility, as you thoughtfully consider how to balance children's needs with families' beliefs.

Every complex-client case is different, so the final outcome will always depend on the situation. You will find that these cases can all be addressed using the process modeled in this chapter. Always begin the process of making a decision by considering whether honoring the family's request could result in harm to a child. Looking back at two of the cases presented here, note that in The Nap case, Chase could be harmed if not given the opportunity to nap because he would be deprived of meeting a basic physiological need. We have presented this case many times, and those who have addressed it have always agreed unanimously (although usually after long deliberation) that the ethical early childhood educator should deny the mother's request if she is convinced that honoring it would be harmful to the child. In the Messy Play case, on the other hand, if efforts to finesse the issue are not successful, the teacher would be justified in granting this mother's request because the costs of restricting the child's access to messy play, at least for the time being, are outweighed by the potential benefits of strengthening the relationship with her mother.

Remember that taking the concerns of family members seriously does not mean that you should agree to all of their requests without considering the impact on their child and the other children in your care. You are a professional who has received training in child development and early childhood education. You should not be arrogant about asserting your expertise, nor should you be so humble that you fail to utilize your specialized knowledge. The Code makes it clear that you have a responsibility to share your knowledge with families to help them better understand their young children.

> I-2.8—To help family members enhance their understanding of their children, as staff are enhancing their understanding of each child through communications with families, and support family members in the continuing development of their skills as parents.

Teaching and directing often involve finding a balance between respecting the wishes of families and ensuring that all children's needs are met. If you are respectful of family members and build good relationships with them from the beginning, they are more likely to understand that all of their requests cannot be accommodated. They will also be appreciative when you honor their requests after careful deliberation, even if you could justify denying them.

6

Ethical Responsibilities to Colleagues

In a caring, cooperative workplace, human dignity is respected, professional satisfaction is promoted, and positive relationships are developed and sustained. Based upon our core values, our primary responsibility to colleagues is to establish and maintain settings and relationships that support productive work and meet professional needs. The same ideals that apply to children also apply as we interact with adults in the workplace.

—NAEYC Code of Ethical Conduct

The third section of the NAEYC Code of Ethical Conduct focuses on the relationships among the adults in early care and education settings and spells out your ethical obligations to your coworkers and employers. This section of the Code is based on the premise that workplace relationships are important and that working in supportive, collegial settings enhances early childhood educators' ability to provide high-quality education and care for children and establish trusting relationships with families.

Ideals

Six Ideals in the NAEYC Code of Ethical Conduct specifically address your ethical responsibilities to coworkers and employers (see page 132 in Appendix B). They cover issues such as confidentiality, collaboration, and recognition of professional achievement.

The third section of the administrator supplement addresses directors' responsibility to cultivate a caring, cooperative work environment and support staff in their professional development (see page 139 in Appendix C). The fourth section identifies directors' responsibilities to sponsoring agencies and governing bodies (see pages 140–141 in Appendix C).

approach and do everything in her power to persuade Vanessa that she needs to stay on task. The next time Vanessa turns her attention away from the children, she explains that it was an emergency and won't happen again. But the next day Vanessa texts on her phone for a long time. Thinking carefully about how to communicate her concerns to Vanessa in a respectful, nonaccusatory way, Takisha says, "You were texting during class time again today. Is everything okay? Is there anything I can do to help you out?"

Takisha then points out calmly that it is difficult for one person to handle the whole group and that she worries about the children's safety and the quality of their experiences. She reminds Vanessa that licensing requires that they have an appropriate number of adults supervising the group at all times. She suggests that if Vanessa must turn her attention away from the children, she should ask the director to find someone to take her place so she can leave the room.

Takisha hopes that being patient, supportive, and straightforward with Vanessa about her concerns will help her see the potential risks she creates for the children and will motivate her to find a better time to deal with personal matters.

4. Look for Guidance in the NAEYC Code

Once it is clear that her efforts have not led Vanessa to change her behavior, Takisha consults the NAEYC Code to gain some insight into how she might address this situation.

She begins with the Core Values and sees that two apply:

- Respect the dignity, worth, and uniqueness of each individual (child, family member, and colleague)
- Recognize that children and adults achieve their full potential in the context of relationships that are based on trust and respect

She then turns to Section I, which describes her obligations to children. She notes that the following Principle would apply if she is concerned that she would not be able to handle an emergency while supervising a group of 20 children virtually alone:

> P-1.1—We shall not harm children. We shall not participate in practices that are emotionally damaging, physically harmful, disrespectful, degrading, dangerous, exploitative, or intimidating to children. **This principle has precedence over all others in this Code**.

She notes that this Ideal also applies:

> I-1.5—To create and maintain safe and healthy settings that foster children's social, emotional, cognitive, and physical development and that respect their dignity and their contributions.

Takisha next turns to the Section III of the Code, which addresses responsibilities to colleagues, and finds two items that are directly relevant to her responsibilities to her coworker.

I-3A.1—To establish and maintain relationships of respect, trust, confidentiality, collaboration, and cooperation with coworkers.

P-3A.2—When we have concerns about the professional behavior of a coworker, we shall first let that person know of our concern in a way that shows respect for personal dignity and for the diversity to be found among staff members, and then attempt to resolve the matter collegially and in a confidential manner.

Finally, Takisha turns to items that address her responsibilities to her employer, which include

I-3B.1—To assist the program in providing the highest quality of service.

She notes, in particular, two items that would provide justification for taking this issue to the director if Vanessa continues to ignore her responsibilities:

P-3B.4—If we have concerns about a colleague's behavior, and children's well-being is not at risk, we may address the concern with that individual. If children are at risk or the situation does not improve after it has been brought to the colleague's attention, we shall report the colleague's unethical or incompetent behavior to an appropriate authority.

P-3B.5—When we have a concern about circumstances or conditions that impact the quality of care and education within the program, we shall inform the program's administration or, when necessary, other appropriate authorities.

5. Decide on a Justifiable Course of Action

In many situations, a colleague approached in a supportive way would recognize the possible consequences of her behavior and would refrain from conducting personal business at work. In other instances, the coworker may become defensive and unwilling to change the behavior. Takisha knows that if this happens, she will need to find another course of action.

Soon after their discussion, Vanessa is again on her phone for a long period. Based on the Code's guidance regarding relationships with coworkers, Takisha makes another good-faith effort to reach a collegial resolution. Again she expresses her concerns about the safety issues involved when one person must supervise 20 children without assistance and points out that if this behavior persists, she will have to share her concern with the director. Vanessa says she understands and promises it won't happen again.

Two weeks later Vanessa is back to texting on her phone without offering an explanation. Takisha knows she cannot keep turning a blind eye to her colleague's behavior. Failing to act would violate her responsibility to ensure children's welfare and the program's commitment to providing quality programming. Because her attempts at a collegial resolution have been unsuccessful, Takisha reports what has been happening to the program director.

The director, familiar with the Supplement for Early Childhood Program Administrators, notes that P-3.10 provides the guidance she needs for this situation: "We shall provide guidance, additional professional development, and coaching for staff whose practices are not appropriate. In instances in which a staff member cannot satisfy reasonable expectations for practice, we shall counsel the staff member to pursue a more appropriate position." She meets with Vanessa, who tells her that she has been dealing with a personal issue that requires her frequent attention. The director acknowledges the stress she is under, but she emphasizes how important it is that Vanessa devote her full attention to the children while working. If she learns that Vanessa is unavailable to the children again, she says, Vanessa will need to seek other employment.

> **Do you believe Takisha was justified in telling the director that Vanessa had not been attending to the children? Do you think it was easy for Takisha to do this? What would you have done in this situation?**

Policy Implications

It is helpful in this type of situation if the program's staff manual reminds employees that they must maintain the required adult–child ratios at all times; failing to do so puts the program out of compliance with licensing regulations. These policies should make it clear that it is not enough for teachers to simply be physically present. Their full attention must be on the children at all times. For this reason, program policies should prohibit the use of smartphones for personal business while teachers are on duty in the classroom except in emergency situations. When the staff manual includes these kinds of specific guidelines, it is easier for a director to address any lapses that occur.

Case 10: Teacher Talk

Several early childhood educators have gathered in the staff room of their program, preparing class materials and drinking coffee. They include Natasha, a kindergarten teacher; Caitlin, the Title I resource teacher; and Deborah, the kindergarten teacher in the room next to Natasha's. Natasha and Caitlin learned that morning that the father of Logan, a child in Natasha's class with whom Caitlin works on a regular basis, had a big fight with Logan's mother and moved out of the house.

"What's the matter with Logan today?" asks Deborah. "He's a terror. The whole time he was on the playground, he was picking a fight with some other child."

"It's not surprising," says Caitlin. "You won't believe what his father did this time. Logan's mother told Natasha and me this morning."

Caitlin proceeds to relate all the details she heard about the fight between Logan's parents that led to his father's packing his clothes and storming out of the house.

> **What is your reaction to the situation described here? To whom does Natasha have responsibilities? What should she consider in deciding what to do?**

Early childhood educators often find themselves needing to manage and safeguard personal information about families. Sometimes families want to know personal information about another child in the class—the name of the child in a toddler group who bit their own child, for example—or a volunteer asks which children receive free lunch. Other situations, such as this one, involve staff members sharing confidential information about children and families. All of these circumstances require teachers to maintain confidentiality and share information strictly on a need-to-know basis.

Determine the Nature of the Problem

This situation is similar to the one in the Personal Business case, in which the teacher had to consider how to respond when her colleague neglected her professional responsibilities. Natasha must decide what, if anything, to say to Caitlin, who has failed to live up to her ethical responsibility to protect this family's privacy. Natasha is facing an ethical dilemma; she has to weigh and balance her obligations to the family with her responsibility to maintain a good relationship with her colleague.

1. Identify the Conflicting Responsibilities

Natasha knows that gossip, particularly this kind of casual talk about families' personal affairs, is commonplace, but that doesn't mean it's harmless. Natasha is concerned that Caitlin's behavior has violated the center's responsibility to respect the family's privacy and fears that someone might unwittingly mention what they have heard to Logan's mother and damage both teachers' relationships with her. Natasha realizes that Caitlin may have thought that sharing this information might help other teachers be more accepting of Logan's behavior during this stressful period.

What Natasha needs to consider is how to help her coworker understand that she shouldn't gossip about families—it breaches her ethical responsibilities and can damage her working relationship with families and colleagues. Natasha wants to help Caitlin become more sensitive to her obligation to hold privileged information in confidence. At the same time, she wants to maintain their good relationship. Natasha must sort out her responsibilities both to Logan's family and to her colleague Caitlin.

2. Brainstorm Possible Resolutions

Natasha's alternatives are to ignore the unprofessional behavior or to address it in some way. Ignoring the behavior does not resolve the situation, but it does preserve her relationship with Caitlin.

3. Consider Ethical Finesse

This situation lends itself to ethical finesse. Since Natasha has a good relationship with Caitlin, she gently and respectfully reminds her of their professional responsibility to keep privileged information confidential. She says, "Caitlin, I'm not comfortable hearing you talk about the children's private family matters with others. I wouldn't want anyone sharing such personal information about me." She hopes such a simple reminder is enough to lead Caitlin and nearby colleagues into other school talk and away from gossip.

Natasha also mentally rehearses other points she could make if Caitlin or other teachers persist in indiscriminately sharing personal information about families. She realizes that having a copy of the Code handy could be helpful to illustrate that the admonition to avoid gossip comes from an important Principle that guides all early childhood educators and is not just her own opinion or preference.

4. Look for Guidance in the NAEYC Code

Like Takisha in the previous case, Natasha is guided by two of the Code's Core Values:

- Respect the dignity, worth, and uniqueness of each individual
- Recognize that children and adults achieve their full potential in the context of relationships that are based on trust and respect

Even though this situation involves Natasha's relationship with her colleague, she begins by referring to Section II of the Code, which addresses her responsibilities to families. She finds the two items listed below to help guide her decision making, noticing that the following explicitly address her situation:

> I-2.2—To develop relationships of mutual trust and create partnerships with the families we serve.

P-2.13—We shall maintain confidentiality and shall respect the family's right to privacy, refraining from disclosure of confidential information and intrusion into family life.

Natasha then turns to the third section of the Code, which addresses her responsibilities to coworkers, for guidance about how to respond to Caitlin. She finds that the same two items that guided Takisha's thinking in the case described above can also help her:

I-3A.1—To establish and maintain relationships of respect [and] trust ... with coworkers.

P-3A.2—When we have concerns about the professional behavior of a coworker, we shall first let that person know of our concern.

While the same items in the Code pertain to Natasha's and Takisha's dilemmas, their situations are somewhat different. Takisha's issue directly impacts the welfare of the children. In addition, it developed over a period of time so she had opportunities to refer to the Code and plan how she would address her concerns with Vanessa. Natasha needs to be ready to respond immediately if she hears more idle gossip because failing to speak up would make it appear that she condones this kind of talk. One reason it is so important for early childhood educators to be familiar with the Code is that they often need to respond quickly to a situation.

5. Decide on a Justifiable Course of Action

The next week Natasha overhears Caitlin relating the story of the family fight to a volunteer who has commented on Logan's disruptive behavior. Natasha is troubled by her colleague's continuing disregard for this family's privacy. She decides to go to Caitlin's classroom after school to address her concerns directly. She hopes that their long-standing relationship will not suffer and that Caitlin will understand her obligation to maintain confidentiality in the future.

Natasha does not feel that it is worth jeopardizing her relationship with Caitlin by reporting the behavior, but she does decide that she needs to do something to help her colleague remember the obligation to refrain from sharing personal information about families in inappropriate ways. She makes an appointment to see the principal and tells her that she has been hearing some gossip in the school and thinks that it might be helpful if she provided the staff with a reminder about professionals' obligation to maintain confidentiality.

After Natasha leaves her office, the principal turns to the Supplement for Early Childhood Program Administrators and finds P-1.3: "We shall have clearly stated policies for the respectful treatment of children and adults in all contacts made by staff, parents, volunteers, student teachers, and other adults. We shall appropriately address incidents that are not consistent with our policies." The principal later tells Natasha that she will bring the topic up at the next staff meeting and also look into providing an ethics workshop for the entire staff in the near future.

Think About this Ethical Dilemma

Natasha's problem is one many early childhood educators face. What is legitimate talk among teachers, and what is idle gossip? In the case of Logan's family, for example, it might have been appropriate for Caitlin to provide general information, such as "Logan's family is going through a difficult time, and his behavior might show that he is under stress." Caitlin crossed the line by sharing all the details of what she heard about the family's personal situation. It may be appropriate to tell colleagues facts that will help them meet a child's needs, but teachers must be very mindful not to betray confidences or share sensitive information indiscriminately. Sharing the specifics about Logan's parents' argument, particularly with a school volunteer, was certainly not acceptable.

> **?** Does Natasha's decision to talk collegially with Caitlin make sense in this situation? Do you think it was appropriate for her to express a general concern to the principal rather than give specific information? What would you have done?

Policy Implications

Maintaining confidentiality (not sharing information obtained in professional practice except under clearly defined circumstances) is an essential moral commitment of every profession. Honoring this commitment is particularly important in early childhood settings because you can learn a great deal about the personal lives of children and their families in the course of your work.

Confidentiality is more easily maintained when programs and schools establish policies to address how sensitive information should be handled. Natasha may have had an easier time handling her situation if she could have referred to clear school policies that were well known to everyone connected with the school—teachers, support staff, administrators, volunteers, and families.

The sample guidelines that follow are firmly grounded in the Code and may help programs develop policies that address the important question "Who needs to know?"

- We will not disclose personal information (such as address, economic status, health status, or family structure) about children or families to other families or those outside the school without permission from a family member or a court order.
- We will not discuss a child or family in a way that makes their identity obvious when a third party is present or when in a public location.
- We will not share information about a child or family or post recognizable photographs of children on any form of social media.
- We will not share sensitive information given to us by a family member without that individual's permission (unless there is a risk to the child).

- Information about a family or child shared with staff should be limited to what they need to know to provide quality services for children.

All staff members should be made aware of the program's confidentiality guidelines.

Another Issue Related to Teacher Talk

What is the best response when a colleague or group of colleagues expresses prejudice or tells inappropriate jokes about a group of children or families? Like the situation in the Personal Business case, this puts a teacher in the uncomfortable position of having to choose between being silent to preserve harmonious relationships with colleagues and speaking up because she feels that expressing prejudice in the workplace is unprofessional and inappropriate. If the teacher chose to respond in this kind of situation, she could say something like "It's disrespectful to tell a joke that ridicules some children and their families. I hope our center is welcoming to all families, so let's keep our conversations more positive and professional."

Case 11: No Hugging

Jayzen just turned 5 and has recently started kindergarten in a public school. He cries and screams every morning when his mother leaves. His teacher, Lily, has found that the transition goes more smoothly when she hugs and soothes him.

The principal has told the school's staff that, to avoid lawsuits that accuse them of touching students inappropriately, they should not hug or touch the children in any way. This advice has been repeated at several faculty meetings, and Lily has also heard him telling individual teachers that hugging children is inappropriate and should be avoided. But Lily knows this no-touching policy is not official; it is not included in any of the staff manuals she has been given. Moreover, she has seen that a hug can help Jayzen make a better transition to school in the morning.

> **What is your first reaction to this situation? Do you think Lily should ignore what the principal has said and give the child the comforting physical touch she believes he needs? Or should she follow the unwritten policy he has established?**

At some time in your career you may be expected to implement practices you believe are not in children's best interests. It could be a policy, an approach to curriculum, or guidance that you think is not developmentally appropriate or beneficial to children. These situations should take you first to the Code's Core Values, then to the items in the Code that identify your interactions with children and families, and then to the items that guide your relationships with colleagues (other teachers and administrators).

Lily knows that physical contact between teachers and students has become a sensitive issue in many schools, but she also knows how comforting a hug or a pat on the back can be in times of stress. She is committed to finding a way to support Jayzen because there may be something serious underlying his behavior, such as toxic stress due to events at home, and she feels it is disrespectful and potentially emotionally damaging to ignore his distress.

Determine the Nature of the Problem

This situation has an ethical dimension because it would be right for Lily to hug Jayzen to comfort him but also right to do what her principal asks the teachers to do. She is facing an ethical dilemma that will require her to decide which of these conflicting courses of action she will choose.

1. Identify the Conflicting Responsibilities

Lily has an obligation to provide Jayzen an emotionally supportive environment that reflects her knowledge of child development research. She also has an obligation to her principal to abide by school policies, one of which prohibits her from providing physical comfort to her students.

2. Brainstorm Possible Resolutions

Lily identifies three potential courses of action. The first option is to defy her principal and continue to comfort Jayzen by hugging him when he is distressed. The second is to follow her principal's instructions and stop hugging or giving Jayzen any physical reassurance when he is upset. And third, she could finesse the dilemma by finding an alternative way to provide Jayzen with the emotional support he needs to transition into the school day.

> **?** Have you ever had to decide whether to follow a directive you thought was unjustified or not in the children's best interest? What did you do? What was the result?

3. Consider Ethical Finesse

Lily can use finesse in this situation by finding another way to provide Jayzen the support he needs. She could encourage a classmate to console him when he's upset or offer him a stuffed animal to hug as he comes into the classroom. It may also help if he has a picture of his family to comfort him. She hopes that one of these strategies will work so that she does not have to decide whether to disregard her principal's prohibition of hugging or giving children other forms of physical reassurance.

She will also share professional literature on this topic with the principal in hopes of convincing him to change his policy.

4. Look for Guidance in the NAEYC Code

When Lily recognizes that her attempts to find an alternative to hugging Jayzen have not been successful, she turns to the NAEYC Code for guidance. She finds three Core Values that apply to this dilemma:

- Base our work on knowledge of how children develop and learn
- Respect the dignity, worth, and uniqueness of each individual (child, family member, and colleague)
- Recognize that children and adults achieve their full potential in the context of relationships that are based on trust and respect

She then turns to Section I, which describes her responsibilities to children. In addition to P-1.1, which prohibits practices that are emotionally damaging, disrespectful, or degrading, she is reminded that she is responsible for promoting children's healthy development:

I-1.2—To base program practices upon current knowledge and research in the field of early childhood education, child development, and related disciplines, as well as on particular knowledge of each child.

I-1.5—To create and maintain safe and healthy settings that foster children's social, emotional, cognitive, and physical development and that respect their dignity and their contributions.

P-1.2—We shall care for and educate children in positive emotional and social environments that are cognitively stimulating and that support each child's culture, language, ethnicity, and family structure.

Section II of the Code addresses Lily's responsibilities to families. These items guide her to help Jayzen's family support him during his transition to school.

I-2.1—To be familiar with the knowledge base related to working effectively with families and to stay informed through continuing education and training.

I-2.8—To help family members enhance their understanding of their children, as staff are enhancing their understanding of each child through communications with families, and support family members in the continuing development of their skills as parents.

Items in Section III of the Code address Lily's responsibilities to her employer:

I-3B.1—To assist the program in providing the highest quality of service.

P-3B.1—We shall follow all program policies. When we do not agree with program policies, we shall attempt to effect change though constructive action within the organization.

5. Decide on a Justifiable Course of Action

When the principal refuses to change this policy, Lily reads the field's professional literature to help her decide how best to resolve this dilemma. She finds journal articles and textbook entries about the important role of physical contact in children's development that support her decision to make Jayzen's well-being her first priority.

Based on this research as well as her observations that Jayzen is comforted by physical reassurance, Lily decides that, at least for the foreseeable future, she will hug Jayzen, pat his back, and even console him in her lap if that is what he needs. She views this approach as an individualized adaptation based on his particular needs. Her goal is to create a positive emotional school environment for him that will set the stage for his future school success.

She plans to share this decision with his parents to strengthen her relationship with them and to help them better understand the importance of making this transition to school a positive, supportive experience.

She has not made the decision to ignore her principal's directive lightly. She knows she has a responsibility to follow the school's policies, but she believes the unwritten no-touching rule is detrimental to children.

> **?** What do you think about Lily's decision? Have you had, or would you have, the courage to oppose a rule you thought was harmful to children? How might her approach have been different if this had been a formal policy included in the employee handbook?

Policy Implications

It appears that Lily's principal made this policy on his own, because it is not in any of the school's handbooks or guidelines. This situation highlights how important it is to base all policies on sound research rather than on personal opinion or in reaction to news stories that sometimes sensationalize issues.

Other Situations that Involve Administrative Directives

A number of other situations involving administrative directives have been reported to us by teachers. Some teachers have been told to implement a scripted curriculum that clashes with children's cultures and home lives and requires that they spend a significant part of each day listening to their teachers and completing worksheets. Other teachers have encountered administrators who have enforced a strict "three strikes and you're out" approach to discipline, leading to widespread expulsions. One program disenrolled children who had more than a predetermined number of toileting accidents. The Code offers helpful guidance when teachers face pressure to do things they believe are detrimental, but it is not easy to confront administrators who enforce policies that violate what teachers know is best for children. The Code directs educators who face this challenge to make constructive efforts to change rules and policies in their programs that are not supported by the field's research on children's learning and development.

Case 12: Difficult Working Relationship

Charity and Nadeen are coteachers of a group of twenty 3- and 4-year-olds in a private preschool program. Charity is in her second year of teaching, and Nadeen has worked in the program for more than 20 years. They have been assigned to work together because the group is larger than in recent years and the director believes this arrangement will best meet these children's needs. Before school starts, Charity and Nadeen meet to discuss their roles in the classroom. After the first month of school, it is clear to Charity that the collaboration is not going well. She feels she is not being treated as a full partner in planning the daily program or in interacting with families.

Charity meets with Nadeen and says she would like to take a more active role in the classroom and in interacting with families. Nadeen does not indicate that she values Charity's expertise or that she will give Charity more opportunities to be involved in planning or working with families. Moreover, after their meeting Charity learns that Nadeen has been gossiping about her with families and staff members and has posted unfavorable comments about her on social media.

Charity tries to be patient, but Nadeen continues to shoulder the planning and teaching responsibilities and to undermine Charity's efforts to develop meaningful relationships with the children's families. After several months, Charity realizes that she needs help. She schedules a meeting with the director, who assures her that Nadeen has taught successfully in the school for a long time and that she is sure the teachers can find ways to work out their differences. Charity is increasingly stressed and unhappy about the situation. She thinks about quitting and finding a job in a more congenial setting, but she does not want to give up. She has good relationships with the children, some of whom are very attached to her, and she does not want to leave them.

> **What is your first reaction? To whom does Charity have obligations? What should she consider when deciding whether to continue to work with Nadeen or resign this position and find another job?**

This case involves a common situation—a teacher's unfair treatment from a colleague. It was discussed in a Focus on Ethics column in *Young Children* (Feeney & Freeman 2015) that featured guest editor Ingrid Anderson. The discussion was informed by commentary from students in early childhood education classes at the University of Hawaii at Mānoa and Portland Community College and by teachers, administrators, and child development specialists who responded to the article after its publication in *Young Children*.

Determine the Nature of the Problem

This situation involves ethics because Charity must decide on a course of action that is right for everyone involved. She has found it very difficult to balance her responsibilities to the children, their families, and her employer; to maintain a collegial relationship with her coteacher; and to address the negative impact of her current working conditions on her own well-being.

Charity recognizes that this is an ethical dilemma. She sees that there is more than one defensible way to balance the conflicting responsibilities created by Nadeen's refusal to give her an equal role in planning and implementing their classroom's curriculum and in working with the families.

1. Identify the Conflicting Responsibilities

Charity knows her first responsibility is to the children. She wants to ensure their physical and emotional safety and support their development and learning. She is afraid that her strained working relationship with Nadeen has had a negative effect on the quality of the children's day-to-day experiences, creating a classroom that is less relaxed and comfortable than it would be if the teachers were true partners.

Charity is also mindful of her responsibilities to the children's families to provide a high-quality program. She realizes that because she has not been able to forge a strong partnership with Nadeen, the program does not live up to the quality she would like to provide.

Although Charity is aware that she also has a responsibility to Nadeen to be a competent and supportive colleague, she believes that Nadeen's treatment of her has made that hard to achieve.

Charity realizes that she has yet another responsibility, one that is not addressed in the Code: to maintain her own personal and professional well-being.

2. Brainstorm Possible Resolutions

The ideal outcome to this dilemma would be for Charity to find a way to make her partnership with Nadeen more equitable. She can also talk to the director again in hopes that she will intervene in the situation or move Charity to another classroom that would be more collegial. The final options are not very attractive—she can put up with the discomfort for the sake of the children or resign from her position and seek other employment.

> **?** Have you ever been in a situation where you could not work effectively with a colleague or you were treated unfairly? What did you do? How was the situation resolved?

3. Consider Ethical Finesse

Charity decides to try to use ethical finesse in an effort to come to an amicable resolution. She approaches Nadeen again and presents the issues to her in a way that focuses on finding a way for the two of them to work together to provide the best possible experiences for the children. When this approach once again fails to change Nadeen's behavior toward Charity in and beyond the classroom, she moves on to other ways to address the issues.

4. Look for Guidance in the NAEYC Code

Charity must make a difficult decision that needs to be well supported by the NAEYC Code of Ethical Conduct. These Core Values help Charity remember to keep first things first:

- Respect the dignity, worth, and uniqueness of each individual (child, family member, and colleague)
- Recognize that children and adults achieve their full potential in the context of relationships that are based on trust and respect

Charity also reviews the Code's items relating to her responsibilities to children:

> I-1.5—To create and maintain safe and healthy settings that foster children's social, emotional, cognitive, and physical development and that respect their dignity and their contributions.

> P-1.2—We shall care for and educate children in positive emotional and social environments that are cognitively stimulating and that support each child's culture, language, ethnicity, and family structure.

Next, she identifies items that address her responsibility to her colleagues and her employer:

> I-3A.1—To establish and maintain relationships of respect, trust, confidentiality, collaboration, and cooperation with coworkers.

> I-3B.1—To assist the program in providing the highest quality of service.

> P-3B.5—When we have a concern about circumstances or conditions that impact the quality of care and education within the program, we shall inform the program's administration or, when necessary, other appropriate authorities.

She also reads this Ideal related to community and society that has relevance to her situation:

> I-4.1—To provide the community with high-quality early childhood care and education programs and services.

5. Decide on a Justifiable Course of Action

Charity decides that I-1.5 and P-1.2 apply to this situation because the strained working relationship and resulting poor communication between the teachers diminish the quality of the program for children.

Charity knows she cannot continue to work in a program where teamwork is impossible and she is treated disrespectfully. But she is not ready to leave until she explores every alternative. Since the discussion with Nadeen did not help the situation, she decides to be guided by P-3B.5 and have another talk with the director. In the meeting, she outlines the steps she has taken in her attempts to improve her working relationship with Nadeen. She clearly explains that even though her reputation in the community is at stake because of Nadeen's disparaging remarks, her primary concerns are the children's experiences and the program's quality. She asks the director to talk with Nadeen about changing the way she interacts with Charity or to consider moving Charity to another classroom.

When the director refuses to intervene with Nadeen and explains that it is not possible to move Charity to another classroom, Charity decides that she needs to take into account her own personal and professional well-being. She decides she must resign and seek employment in a setting that is more collegial, honors her professional expertise, and allows her to better meet the needs of children.

> **?** Do you believe Charity's decision to resign her position is justified because of how she has been treated by her colleague and by the director? What would you have done if you were in her place?

Reflection on Situations that Involve Teacher Relationships

This case struck a familiar chord for a number of teachers who participated in the classes and workshops where it was presented and for those who responded to the article in *Young Children*. It generated a good deal of lively discussion. Respondents pointed out that new teachers are likely to find it particularly difficult to initiate the kind of sensitive conversations called for in this situation. They are inclined to feel they are not in a position to speak up, and many find it easier to ignore a colleague's abusive behavior than to confront it. An additional issue that was raised was that of the imbalance of power present in many centers, particularly when teachers do not feel supported by their administrators.

Ingrid Anderson, who edited this case in the Focus on Ethics column, pointed out that this scenario was particularly difficult to navigate because of the tension between the good of the classroom and school community and the teacher's well-being. It raises an important issue: At what point does our ethical responsibility to children, families, and our programs stop and responsibility to ourselves become a priority?

Citing research findings that early childhood educators often sacrifice their own well-being to serve the children in their care (Anderson 2014; Osgood 2010), Ingrid concluded the column with the reminder that when we fail to care for ourselves, we increase our stress and decrease our resiliency. This makes us vulnerable and compromises our ability to provide the best possible care and education for children. Mindfulness, reflective practice, and paying attention to our work require a strong, resilient self.

This case and others that put dedicated teachers in the situation of either staying in a position they find difficult or leaving the position—or even the field of education—remind us that we have important responsibilities to ourselves and our own well-being. This issue has not, to date, been addressed in the NAEYC Code, but it bears careful thought and examination and may be considered the next time the Code undergoes review and revision.

7

Ethical Responsibilities to Community and Society

Early childhood programs operate within the context of their immediate community made up of families and other institutions concerned with children's welfare. Our responsibilities to the community are to provide programs that meet the diverse needs of families, to cooperate with agencies and professions that share the responsibility for children, to assist families in gaining access to those agencies and allied professionals, and to assist in the development of community programs that are needed but not currently available.

—NAEYC Code of Ethical Conduct

Most people are not specialists in child development and early childhood education, so they count on those with that expertise to nurture children's learning and development and to support their families. For that reason, the fourth and last section of the NAEYC Code of Ethical Conduct addresses early childhood educators' ethical obligations to their communities and to society. It is the most far-reaching and idealistic portion of the Code.

This section of the Code encourages you to use your knowledge and expertise, and to work with others in the field, to serve your community and society. On the individual level, it addresses interactions with your community's resources and institutions, including the agencies and professionals who evaluate children for special education services and those who investigate suspected child abuse and neglect. It directs you to take action when those responsible for children's welfare do not provide the services needed or adequately protect children's safety and well-being. This section of the Code also urges you to work with others and look beyond the walls of your classroom and program to join the field's efforts to make the world a better place for young children.

The final section of the administrator supplement addresses the director's role as a leader in the program's efforts to engage with, and provide leadership to, programs serving young children in their community and beyond. It encourages administrators to use their knowledge and expertise to promote quality programming and services that enhance the well-being of young children and their families.

By leading collective efforts focused on the important social value of ensuring all children's well-being, the field satisfies one hallmark of a profession—altruism. Not every early childhood educator, at every stage of her professional journey, is expected to engage in collective advocacy, but it is important that the field as a whole accept its responsibility to act and advocate on behalf of young children and their families.

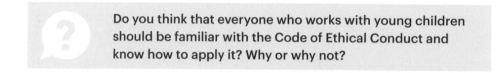

Do you think that everyone who works with young children should be familiar with the Code of Ethical Conduct and know how to apply it? Why or why not?

Ideals

The eight Ideals in the fourth section of the Code describe your responsibilities to your community and society and address the field's concern for all children's welfare (see page 133 in Appendix B). The Ideals encourage educators to be personally committed to providing high-quality services while working with professionals and agencies to ensure the safety and well-being of children, families, and colleagues. They also promote appropriate assessment practices and the field's increased professionalism and commitment to the Core Values identified in the Code.

Ideals in the final section of the administrator supplement call on directors to increase the public's awareness about the importance of high-quality early learning programming; serve the community by being a resource, spokesperson, and advocate for children, families, and quality programs; and strengthen the field's commitment to the Code and the administrator supplement (see page 141 in Appendix C).

Principles

The 13 Principles in the fourth section of the Code address early childhood educators' individual and collective obligations to their community and society. These obligations include accurately describing the program and the services provided; accepting only positions for which you are qualified; and upholding laws and regulations that promote children's welfare while working to change policies or practices that are inappropriate or could be harmful to children (see pages 133–134 in Appendix B).

The administrator supplement includes 14 Principles that address directors' responsibilities to the community, society, and the field (see pages 141–142 in Appendix C). They cover issues such as the importance of holding staff accountable for following applicable laws and regulations and accurately representing the field's stance on best practices.

Typical Ethical Dilemmas Involving Community and Society

Directives that do not reflect best practices for working with young children are often created by entities outside of early childhood programs. Some examples of these are distributing child care subsidies inequitably, permitting harsh discipline of children, not requiring child care programs to test for lead in drinking water, limiting the amount of recess time, and closing centers without sufficient advance notice to families.

The three cases in this chapter address violating licensing regulations and program policies, responding to practices that are detrimental to children's health and safety, working with agencies responsible for protecting children's safety, and addressing local- or state-mandated assessment practices that are contrary to accepted best practices.

Case 13: Violating Licensing Regulations

Theo teaches in a community-based child development center that is part of a national chain. Although the center has some wonderful teachers who are doing exciting things with the children, the program is out of compliance with several state licensing regulations. Playground equipment needs to be repaired, fire drills are held infrequently, rooms are filled beyond the capacity allowed by licensing, and classrooms often do not maintain required adult-to-child ratios. Theo is also aware that the director sometimes gives incomplete or misleading information to state licensing inspectors. He is struggling to know what to do—is he obligated to report the infractions to an inspector or the licensing agency?

> **?** What is your first reaction to this situation? To whom does Theo have obligations? What factors should he take into account when deciding what to do?

Versions of this case were published in *Young Children* as part of our original work on ethics (Feeney 1987) and in the Focus on Ethics column in *Young Children* (Feeney & Freeman 2011). The following discussion incorporates readers' responses and analyses from those articles.

Determine the Nature of the Problem

This situation involves ethics because Theo must determine whether it would be right to report the licensing infractions or to keep his concerns to himself. He could report the infractions to the licensing agency, or he could assume that they are not serious and wait to see if the director corrects them once they are brought to her attention. As Theo explores the situation further, however, he realizes that he is not facing an ethical dilemma; he is facing an ethical responsibility. Because children's welfare is at stake, he must act.

1. Identify the Conflicting Responsibilities

Theo likes working at this center. While his job is gratifying, he is concerned about the large group sizes, the condition of the playground, and the director's disregard for licensing regulations. He turns to the NAEYC Code for guidance. His review of the Code reminds him that his primary responsibility is to ensure the safety of the children. He knows he also has a responsibility to be a good employee and to be loyal to his employer, but she is allowing practices and situations that could endanger the children's welfare. Theo is experiencing a personal conflict as well. He needs his job and fears that he will lose it if he reports his concerns to licensing authorities.

2. Brainstorm Possible Resolutions

Brainstorming alternative resolutions is not an option in this situation. Theo's primary responsibility is to the children at the center. If he is not certain that the licensing violations are going to be corrected immediately, he must report the situation to the authorities.

> **?** Have you encountered a program that has knowingly violated licensing regulations? What steps did you take when you discovered these violations? How can the Code be helpful in that kind of situation?

3. Consider Ethical Finesse

Theo wonders if he can find a way to uphold his responsibility to keep the children safe without having to make a report to authorities. He discusses the situation with other teachers to determine whether they share his concerns and to see if any of them would be willing to join him in talking with the director.

Theo and a colleague approach the director in a friendly and constructive way. They express their concerns and ask what plans she has for bringing the center into full compliance with licensing regulations. If the director responds with genuine concern—proposing specific plans to immediately add more staff to keep class sizes and ratios in compliance, begin repairs on the playground, and conduct regular fire drills—and if she pledges to be totally truthful when talking with the licensing inspector, then finesse will have successfully resolved the problem.

4. Look for Guidance in the NAEYC Code

The director appeared to have listened to the teachers' concerns when they talked to her, but it is soon apparent that no new staff have been hired and that she has not begun to address the safety issues that were discussed.

Theo consults the NAEYC Code again for help in deciding the next steps. He finds no specific guidance in the Core Values, but the Ideals and Principles in the section on Ethical Responsibilities to Children underscore the seriousness of his obligations. As should be done in every situation that affects children's well-being, Theo begins by considering Principle 1.1, which has precedence over all others:

> Above all, we shall not harm children. We shall not participate in practices that are emotionally damaging, physically harmful, disrespectful, degrading, dangerous, exploitative, or intimidating to children.

He finds the following Ideals especially compelling:

> I-1.4—To appreciate the vulnerability of children and their dependence on adults.

> I-1.5—To create and maintain safe and healthy settings that foster children's social, emotional, cognitive, and physical development and that respect their dignity and their contributions.

Theo thinks that, on occasion, being slightly off from the required teacher–child ratios or having groups that are a few children larger than those permitted by licensing regulations is not necessarily harmful to the children, but he worries about what could happen if a child became injured or very ill when there are too few adults supervising a group. He is particularly concerned about the potential for injury on the playground. He realizes that the program is violating these items in the Code's section describing its responsibilities to its community:

> I-4.1—To provide the community with high-quality early childhood care and education programs and services.

> P-4.6—We shall be familiar with laws and regulations that serve to protect the children in our programs and be vigilant in ensuring that these laws and regulations are followed.

By speaking to the director in his attempt to finesse this issue, Theo has addressed two important responsibilities:

> P-3A.2—When we have concerns about the professional behavior of a coworker, we shall first let that person know of our concern in a way that shows respect for personal dignity and for the diversity to be found among staff members, and then attempt to resolve the matter collegially and in a confidential manner.

P-3B.1—We shall follow all program policies. When we do not agree with program policies, we shall attempt to effect change through constructive action within the organization.

And, as he studies the Code, he finds this additional guidance related to his responsibilities to his employer:

I-3B.2—To do nothing that diminishes the reputation of the program in which we work unless it is violating laws and regulations designed to protect children or is violating the provisions of this Code.

P-3B.3—We shall not violate laws or regulations designed to protect children and shall take appropriate action consistent with this Code when aware of such violations.

In the end, Theo finds the Code provides clear guidance about how to address concerns:

P-3B.5—When we have a concern about circumstances or conditions that impact the quality of care and education within the program, we shall inform the program's administration or, when necessary, other appropriate authorities.

P-4.7—When we become aware of a practice or situation that endangers the health, safety, or well-being of children, we have an ethical responsibility to protect children or inform parents and/or others who can.

P-4.8—We shall not participate in practices that are in violation of laws and regulations that protect the children in our programs.

5. Decide on a Justifiable Course of Action

Constructive conversation would often be enough to resolve this kind of situation, but Theo has made that effort and the necessary changes have not occurred. He now realizes that the Code clearly compels him to report problems if the potential exists for children to be harmed. The moral obligation to do no harm to children, as expressed in P-1.1 of the NAEYC Code, confirms his resolve.

He decides to bring the program's licensing violations to the attention of the center's regional office. If he finds no one willing to take immediate action, he plans to contact the child care licensing agency. (Reporting a program's violation of state regulations to an appropriate outside authority is referred to as *whistle-blowing*.)

Theo also decides that if these issues are not addressed at once, he will look for another place of employment. This is a difficult decision because he knows that his leaving will have an impact on the children; even so, he wants to work in a program that is committed to providing good service to the community and makes the welfare of children its highest priority.

> Do you believe Theo was justified in his decision to report violations of licensing regulations? Under what circumstances might a teacher alert the parents to these violations? Are there any circumstances under which any early childhood educator should work in a program that violates state regulations and the provisions of the NAEYC Code?

Policy Implications

Many programs include the NAEYC Code in their employee and family handbooks and make it clear that all employees, without exception, are to follow its mandates. If that were the case in this program, the director might have realized that she was violating the provisions of the Code and the law and felt compelled to immediately make the necessary changes.

Case 14: Ineffective Child Protective Services Agency

Constance is an experienced teacher and aware of her obligations to report suspected child abuse to the local child protective services agency. This responsibility is addressed in the policies and procedures manual of her center and is consistent with state laws. The last time she reported her suspicion of abuse to this agency, however, the caseworker visited the family but did not promptly intervene. That family left town immediately after the caseworker's visit and was not heard from again. Constance is once again concerned that a child in her class is being abused. She has seen severe bruises on 3-year-old Gina's arms and legs and has noticed that she is anxious and fearful. Constance has also heard that the child's mother is afraid of Gina's father's quick and violent temper.

> What is your first reaction to this case? To whom does Constance have obligations? What factors should she take into account when making a decision about what to do?

Your responsibility to report suspected child abuse or neglect is addressed in Section I of the Code and discussed in the Suspected Child Abuse case in Chapter 4. This situation is different from that one, however, because it involves concerns about the community agency that is responsible for children's welfare and has shown itself to be ineffective in protecting children.

Determine the Nature of the Problem

This situation involves ethics since a child's welfare is involved. Constance has a legal mandate and an ethical responsibility to report her suspicion of abuse. She has an additional ethical responsibility to follow up to make sure that the child protection agency is doing everything possible to protect Gina from further harm. This extra effort is particularly important because of the concerns Constance has about how this agency handled her previous referral. She has a responsibility to work with other advocates to improve the quality of the community's child protective services to protect other children from harm.

1. Identify the Conflicting Responsibilities

Constance knows that she must report the suspected abuse, although she fears that doing so could result in further injury to the child. Principle 1.1 in the NAEYC Code mandates that she take action. But this Principle is at the root of Constance's concern: She realizes that it might not be effective to follow the law and to report suspected child abuse. She fears that by obeying the law, she might put Gina at even more risk.

2. Brainstorm Possible Resolutions

It is not appropriate to brainstorm possible responses in this situation. Constance has good reason to believe that Gina is in danger, and she understands that she must report her suspicion of abuse.

3. Consider Ethical Finesse

Constance cannot finesse this situation—she has to act.

> **?** Have you experienced a situation in which a child protective services agency was not effective in protecting children? What actions did you consider or carry out? What was the outcome?

4. Look for Guidance in the NAEYC Code

Constance knows that the first Principle in the Code requires her to protect Gina from harm.

> P-1.1—Above all, we shall not harm children. We shall not participate in practices that are emotionally damaging, physically harmful, disrespectful, degrading, dangerous, exploitative, or intimidating to children. **This principle has precedence over all others in this Code**.

Constance notes the following Ideals that are relevant to this situation:

I-1.4—To appreciate the vulnerability of children and their dependence on adults.

I-1.5—To create and maintain safe and healthy settings that foster children's social, emotional, cognitive, and physical development and that respect their dignity and their contributions.

I-4.7—To support policies and laws that promote the well-being of children and families, and to work to change those that impair their well-being. To participate in developing policies and laws that are needed, and to cooperate with families and other individuals and groups in these efforts.

She finds that these Principles that address her individual responsibilities to community and society are also applicable:

P-4.6—We shall be familiar with laws and regulations that serve to protect the children in our programs and be vigilant in ensuring that these laws and regulations are followed.

P-4.7—When we become aware of a practice or situation that endangers the health, safety, or well-being of children, we have an ethical responsibility to protect children or inform parents and/or others who can.

P-4.8—We shall not participate in practices that are in violation of laws and regulations that protect the children in our programs.

She also notices that these two collective responsibilities directly address her situation:

P-4.12—When we have evidence that an agency that provides services intended to ensure children's well-being is failing to meet its obligations, we acknowledge a collective ethical responsibility to report the problem to appropriate authorities or to the public. We shall be vigilant in our follow-up until the situation is resolved.

P-4.13—When a child protection agency fails to provide adequate protection for abused or neglected children, we acknowledge a collective ethical responsibility to work toward the improvement of these services.

Working Together to Prevent Child Abuse and Neglect

Agencies and programs that focus on young children can do the following to help prevent child abuse and neglect:

- Provide preservice and in-service education that includes strategies for supporting families, identifying and responding to the symptoms of abuse and neglect, and interpreting ethical responsibilities to children and families.

- Ensure that people entering the field of early care and education receive training in recognizing the signs of possible child abuse and neglect, learn reporting procedures, and understand and use their code of professional ethics.

- Put the spotlight on public education efforts designed to prevent child abuse and neglect.

- Share websites and publications that offer information on preventing child abuse and neglect.

- Work to improve the child protection services available to children and families.

- Work toward changing laws or regulatory services if they are ineffective in protecting children.

- Participate in developing new laws and regulations that improve conditions for children and work to ensure their implementation.

Finally, Constance realizes that she needs to work with other advocates to support the community's efforts to protect vulnerable children:

> I-4.7—To support policies and laws that promote the well-being of children and families, and to work to change those that impair their well-being. To participate in developing policies and laws that are needed, and to cooperate with families and other individuals and groups in these efforts.

5. Decide on a Justifiable Course of Action

Constance cannot think of an alternative that is consistent with her moral and legal obligations and might more effectively protect Gina, so she reports her suspicion that Gina is the victim of abuse. She also talks with Beverly, the center director, who is aware that past reports to the child protective services agency were not promptly addressed. In addition to taking her responsibility for the children's well-being seriously, Beverly always encourages her staff to speak and act in the best interests of the children and their families (supplement I-3.2) and supports them as they carry out their responsibilities (supplement P-3.1). Thus, Constance feels comfortable bringing her concerns about the agency to Beverly.

Constance and Beverly discuss the issue with a supervisor in the child protective services agency, and they try to get an assurance that Gina's case will be handled more effectively. Constance and Beverly follow up by telephone the next day to establish a personal link with the caseworker assigned to work with the family. This step is supported by P-4.12 (above).

Constance is committed to working to make changes in procedures for handling reported child abuse if this referral is not handled properly. She has decided that if she has concerns about how Gina's case is handled she will coordinate with Beverly and other staff to enlist the help of their local Association for the Education of Young Children (AEYC) affiliate and other local child advocates (P-4.12). She will also contact her state legislator to discuss ways she and other advocates might be able to contribute to efforts to improve the protection provided in their community for children who are victims of abuse (I-4.7).

Think About this Ethical Responsibility

This case illustrates that early childhood educators do not operate in a vacuum—they are part of a web of community programs and services designed to meet children's needs and protect them from harm. It further demonstrates that these responsibilities involve more than making appropriate referrals. There is a higher level of obligation to make sure that the agencies responsible are actually doing an effective job of protecting children. The sidebar on page 109 describes some ways you can work to prevent child abuse and neglect.

What is your reaction to Constance's decision? What else could she do to protect Gina? What are your obligations when you have reason to believe that following the law might result in harm to a child?

Case 15: Standardized Testing in Kindergarten

Daniella is a kindergarten teacher at a public primary school in a diverse, mostly low-income community. Third grade reading scores at her school and several others in the district have dropped dramatically in the last few years. The state department of education has put pressure on these schools' administrators and teachers to raise students' scores on the state-mandated reading test. The district has responded to these pressures by requiring kindergarten teachers to administer a standardized reading test to demonstrate that children are making adequate progress toward mastering the material they will be tested on at the end of third grade. This year's test is now just weeks away.

Daniella prides herself on providing meaningful, hands-on learning experiences for her students and helping them feel successful as learners. When she administered the test for the first time last year, the children started the task with enthusiasm, but she soon observed behaviors that convinced her the testing experience was stressful for the children and was undermining their confidence.

Daniella believes that the test's paper-and-pencil format is not appropriate for kindergartners, particularly those who are dual language learners. She knows that for many of her students, the test taking will be stressful and discouraging.

> **What is your first reaction to this issue? To whom does Daniella have responsibilities? What factors should she take into account when deciding how she should respond to this mandate?**

An analysis of this case appeared in the Focus on Ethics column in *Young Children* (Feeney & Freeman 2014b). The predicament described is not unique; the concern that all students meet increasingly rigorous state standards has led many districts to assess what even the youngest children know and are able to do. Daniella must consider both her responsibilities to the children she teaches and those she has to her school and district.

Determine the Nature of the Problem

Daniella's observations have led her to conclude that the required test has the potential to harm children, and she knows she has an ethical obligation to keep these children safe. But she knows that it is also right for her to follow all program policies and to do nothing to diminish the school's reputation, which would surely result if students' scores continue to decline. Daniella concludes that she is, in fact, facing an ethical dilemma: What she thinks is good for the kindergartners she teaches is in conflict with what district administrators are requiring her to do.

1. Identify the Conflicting Responsibilities

In this situation, Daniella must balance her responsibilities of ensuring the well-being of the children with her responsibility to follow district mandates. She does not believe that the test is appropriate for the children she works with or that it will provide teachers with useful information. On the other hand, she is well aware that school and district administrators are taking these test scores very seriously, and she appreciates that as an employee she has an obligation to follow district policies.

2. Brainstorm Possible Resolutions

There are two obvious resolutions to this dilemma. Daniella can honor the requirements and administer the test, or she can refuse to administer it, taking the position that she is a conscientious objector. Refusing to give the test might cost Daniella her job. She loves teaching, and she realizes that this option is not the best for her or for the children. Refusing to give the test is not a viable option for most teachers who work in public schools and want to retain their positions. As the time for administering the test approaches, Daniella is unsure how to proceed.

> **?** Have you ever had to choose between following an employer's mandate and protecting children from harm? What did you do? What resources did you rely on to decide on the best response?

3. Consider Ethical Finesse

Since refusing to administer the test is not a viable alternative, Daniella considers other options. Using data from observing children and research findings about the effects of inappropriate testing on young children, she can advocate for the needs of the children and work to change the policy. This is probably the most feasible course of action in this situation. This action would not meet Daniella's desire to keep the children she is now teaching from taking the test, but it would have the potential to improve the situation for children in the future and preserve Daniella's relationship with her employer.

4. Look for Guidance in the NAEYC Code

The following items in the Code, which apply to appropriate assessment practices and uses, are relevant to Daniella's situation:

> I-1.6—To use assessment instruments and strategies that are appropriate for the children to be assessed, that are used only for the purposes for which they were designed, and that have the potential to benefit children.

I-1.7—To use assessment information to understand and support children's development and learning, to support instruction, and to identify children who may need additional services.

P-1.5—We shall use appropriate assessment systems, which include multiple sources of information, to provide information on children's learning and development.

P-2.7—We shall inform families about the nature and purpose of the program's child assessments and how data about their child will be used.

The following items in the Code apply to advocacy:

I-4.5—To work to ensure that appropriate assessment systems, which include multiple sources of information, are used for purposes that benefit children.

P-4.5—We shall be knowledgeable about the appropriate use of assessment strategies and instruments and interpret results accurately to families.

These items in the Code of Ethical Conduct are consistent with and reinforce NAEYC's joint position statement "Early Childhood Curriculum, Assessment, and Program Evaluation," developed in conjunction with the National Association of Early Childhood Specialists in State Departments of Education (NAECS/SDE). This document states,

Make ethical, appropriate, valid, and reliable assessment a central part of all early childhood programs. To assess young children's strengths, progress, and needs, use assessment methods that are developmentally appropriate, culturally and linguistically responsive, tied to children's daily activities, supported by professional development, inclusive of families, and connected to specific, beneficial purposes: (1) making sound decisions about teaching and learning, (2) identifying significant concerns that may require focused intervention for individual children, and (3) helping programs improve their educational and developmental interventions. (NAEYC & NAECS/SDE 2003, 2)

The items in the NAEYC Code listed above identify important ethical dimensions of assessing young children. In Daniella's case, they underscore the fact that the required assessment does not appear to be designed to benefit children by informing classroom practice. When Daniella looks at these items in conjunction with P-1.1, which states that early childhood educators shall not harm children, she realizes that her concern about administering the test is justified.

While Daniella is concerned that this test may have a negative impact on some children, she is also committed to upholding her responsibilities to her employer as identified in the Code, this item in particular:

P-3B.1—We shall follow all program policies. When we do not agree with program policies, we shall attempt to effect change through constructive action within the organization.

5. Decide on a Justifiable Course of Action

Daniella decides that while she will administer the test, she will also advocate for appropriate assessment practices. She will further research the impact of testing on young children and then talk with her colleagues to see if anyone shares her concerns and wishes to join her in discussing these concerns with the principal. Next, she will let her school principal know what she has learned about potential negative consequences of the test. Then she will consider other actions that may be appropriate. She will do whatever she can to reduce testing and minimize its effects on children.

> **?** How do you feel about Daniella's decision? What would you do if you were in the same situation?

Think About this Ethical Dilemma

We hope that reading this case will encourage you to consider the ethical dimensions of testing the academic achievement of young children. We encourage you to add your voice to those of other advocates committed to ensuring that assessment practices are beneficial for children (see the discussion of how to become an informed advocate on page 115).

Reflection on Cases that Involve Advocacy

The NAEYC Code reminds you of your responsibility to share your specialized knowledge and expertise to ensure young children's safety and well-being. This chapter describes three circumstances that led the teachers involved to commit to taking action on behalf of the young children they teach: Theo decided to report the program where he worked for frequent violations of licensing regulations, Constance and her director made a commitment to follow up on a report of suspected child abuse to be certain the child protection agency handled the report appropriately, and Daniella resolved to advocate for appropriate assessment strategies for kindergarteners. Advocating for young children and their families at the school and community levels and on a larger stage requires you to be well informed and ready to speak up about what you know is best for young children and families.

When you are new to the field, your advocacy is likely to focus on helping families better understand why you teach the way you do. As you become more experienced and gain confidence in expressing what you know is right, you are likely to be better prepared to take an informed position in your center, your community, and sometimes on an even larger scale.

We urge all early childhood educators to be well-informed professionals and to network with others to influence the policies that govern young children's experiences in your school, your community, and beyond.

Becoming an Informed Advocate for Appropriate Assessment

Learn about appropriate assessment

- Review research findings showing that test results may not be valid and reliable due to the difficulty of administering tests to young children. Here are a few resources:
  - » *Early Childhood Assessment: Why, What, and How*, National Research Council (The National Academies Press, 2008). www.nap.edu/catalog/12446/early-childhood-assessment-why-what-and-how
  - » "Early Childhood Curriculum, Assessment, and Program Evaluation" (NAEYC position statement developed in collaboration with NAECS/SDE). NAEYC.org/sites/default/files/globally-shared/downloads/PDFs/resources/position-statements/pscape.pdf
  - » *Developing Kindergarten Readiness and Other Large-Scale Assessment Systems: Necessary Considerations in the Assessment of Young Children*, Kyle Snow (NAEYC, 2011). https://issuu.com/naeyc/docs/assessment_systems
  - » "Using Documentation and Assessment to Support Children's Learning" (*Young Children* cluster issue, Vol. 68, No. 3, July 2013)
  - » "Effective Kindergarten Readiness Assessments: Influencing Policy, Informing Instruction, and Creating Joyful Classrooms" (*Young Children*, Vol. 73, No. 1, March 2018)
  - » Materials from advocacy groups such as the National Black Child Development Institute (www.nbcdi.org) and Defending the Early Years (www.deyproject.org) can help you stay up to date on current developments and get involved in public efforts relating to inappropriate assessments.

Use developmentally appropriate practice in the classroom

- Recognize that children can acquire the knowledge and skills that are required in content standards through engagement with a meaningful, intentionally designed hands-on curriculum.
- Resist the temptation to teach to the test and avoid overemphasizing test-taking skills to the exclusion of other worthwhile content.

Engage in advocacy in your school and community

- Engage in collegial dialogue about testing with fellow teachers and school administrators.
- Articulate your position clearly to let the school community know what you believe and why.
- Join together with others to speak out about appropriate assessment strategies and uses of assessment results.
- Help policy makers understand the risks to young children of inappropriate assessments.
- Write to your local media about the need for appropriate testing practices.
- Present workshops or panels about testing issues at a local AEYC affiliate meeting or a meeting of another association concerned with early childhood education.
- Provide written or oral testimony regarding legislation on testing.
- Help other teachers, families, and community members understand that multiple measures provide a better sense of a child's development and help to shape effective curriculum.

8

The Code of Ethics and You

The Role of Ethics in Early Childhood Education

In Chapter 1 we described a profession as an occupation whose members have special obligations to society. A code of ethical conduct identifies your field's core values, provides a vision for the profession, and guides members' behavior. It complements your personal attributes, values, and morality. A code of ethics

- Increases your ethical awareness and judgment
- Provides a basis for resolving the principal ethical dilemmas you encounter in your work
- Supports you when you take a morally courageous stand
- Helps create a sense of professional identity
- Communicates to those outside the field what they can expect from members of a profession

Since its adoption, the NAEYC Code has promoted the welfare of young children and helped to provide a unified approach to ethics in the many different settings and agencies that provide care and education to young children. It has helped to foster early childhood educators' professional behavior and contributed to the field's efforts to be recognized as a profession.

The Code is used and respected because it represents many voices. Input from NAEYC members has always been a hallmark of the association's work on professional ethics. Members have contributed to the development of the Code and its two supplements, and their input has informed articles and columns about ethical issues. This ongoing participation reflects NAEYC's commitment to being an inclusive and participatory organization. It contributes to the field's efforts to protect children and guides early childhood educators as they balance their responsibilities to children, families, colleagues, and the community.

> **?** How does your knowledge of the NAEYC Code of Ethical Conduct affect the way you view the value of your work? How has the Code contributed to your sense of being a professional?

NAEYC and Ethics

NAEYC supports the application of the Code in many ways. Varied resources are available to help you become more familiar with the Code and use it in your work. The Code is also an integral part of teachers' professional preparation standards and is incorporated into initiatives designed to improve the quality of programs that serve young children.

Publications and Conferences

More than a million brochures of the Code (in English and in Spanish) have been printed and distributed, and the Code and its supplements are available as position statements at NAEYC.org. *Young Children* has frequently published articles focused on the Code. If you are a member, you can access these on the website. Focus on Ethics, a column in *Young Children*, explores ethical dilemmas submitted by NAEYC members, solicits input from readers, and publishes analyses of each of the cases based on reader input. These columns are available to members on the website; nonmembers can access selected columns. NAEYC has also published a number of books on professional ethics, two of which are currently in print and available with up-to-date information that reflects best practices (this volume and *Teaching the NAEYC Code of Ethical Conduct: A Resource Guide*, revised edition [Feeney, Freeman, & Moravcik 2016]).

Consider attending a session at an NAEYC or AEYC affiliate conference that focuses on the Code and its application. Full-day training of trainers sessions on how to teach and apply the Code are also offered at conferences.

Quality Enhancement Initiatives

NAEYC accredits programs serving young children as well as institutions that prepare individuals to work in the field of early childhood education. The Code of Ethical Conduct is an integral part of both of these accreditation systems. Accredited early learning programs must demonstrate that all teaching staff know and use the field's ethical guidelines. Guidelines for NAEYC accreditation of two-year, four-year, and graduate-level teacher education programs, as well as the Child Development Associate (CDA) credential, incorporate core elements of the Code.

The Code is also an essential component of NAEYC's Power to the Profession (P2P) initiative. P2P focuses on building a framework for the early childhood profession to advance a high-quality workforce and a fair compensation structure.

Together, these efforts contribute to practitioners' awareness and knowledge of ethical practice as described in the Code.

The Future of Ethics in Early Childhood Education

Although the Code has existed for more than 40 years, work on ethics is far from over. We envision a future in which all early childhood educators have access to training in ethics that will help them become ever more skilled in using and sharing the Code and gain the confidence to make decisions that safeguard the well-being of children, families, and colleagues. As a well-prepared early childhood professional, commit yourself to helping others, both within and outside the field, and to furthering the field's collective ideals of ensuring high-quality services for every child and advocating for the needs of young children and families.

Working on issues that involve ethics provides a wonderful opportunity for people from different roles and perspectives to focus on shared values and work together to grow in their understanding of their ethical responsibilities. Attention to professional ethics can strengthen the community of early childhood educators and remind us to keep our moral compasses pointed in the direction of what is best for young children. Making the Code a cornerstone of our professional practice communicates our dedication to serving young children and their families and contributes to society's growing appreciation of the increasingly professional early childhood workforce.

Your Future, Your Commitment to the Code

In the first chapter of this book we asked you to identify your personal values and consider the sources of your personal morality. We introduced the core values and professional ethics of the early childhood field and urged you to expand your existing values and morality to include them. In closing, we ask you to reflect on the interaction of your personal values and morality with the NAEYC Code's Core Values, Ideals, and Principles.

Your ethical behavior comes from a concern for the welfare of others, knowledge of the NAEYC Code, and the willingness and ability to reflect on your actions. When you thoughtfully consider morally challenging situations and reflect on possible outcomes, you improve your ability to respond to ethical issues that arise in your work.

The Code will support you in doing what is right for young children and their families. Understanding the Code and using it with thought and care are an ongoing process. You will want to consult the Code often—to remind yourself of your commitments to children, families, colleagues, and the community; for support when you are tempted to do what's easy but not necessarily right; and for guidance in addressing ethical dilemmas.

Caring for the youngest, most vulnerable members of our society, acting on your commitment to doing your work with skill and integrity, and being ethical in your practice challenges and changes you. In caring for others and using your expertise on their behalf, you step outside of yourself and contribute to society. It takes you full circle: Who you are as a person influences the professional you become, and the professional you become influences who you are as a person.

Your belief in the importance of your work will strengthen with your growing understanding of the lifelong impact of your interactions with young children. Your valuing of children as individuals may result in advocacy for all children in our society and in the world. Your personal beliefs, values, and morality may be enriched and extended by the core values and ethics of the field of early childhood education.

NAEYC can take pride in being at the forefront of the work on professional ethics in early childhood education. And you can take pride in being part of it.

> Think about the ways in which your work in early childhood education has affected your personal values and morality. How has the Code influenced your understanding of right and wrong, fair and unfair in working with young children and their families? What can you do to further your commitment to ethical practice?

Reflection Questions

Consider the following questions to continue your thoughtful engagement with what you have learned about professional ethics and the NAEYC Code of Ethical Conduct in this book. If possible, discuss these questions with a partner or in a small group, or use them as a topic for personal reflection and journal writing.

1. Identify some personal values that led you to choose to work with young children. How might these be reflected in your work with children and families?

2. How were your values and morality shaped by your upbringing? In what ways, if any, are they different today from when you were younger? If they are different, why do you think they changed?

3. Whose voice do you hear in your mind when you are faced with a moral issue? What kind of advice might that person give you?

4. Is it possible for two people to be good professionals even if they have very different personal values? Why?

5. What significant social value do you think is promoted by the field of early childhood education?

6. Think of a time you encountered an ethical dilemma (a situation with two defensible resolutions) in your work. What was it? What did you do and what was the outcome?

7. Have you experienced a situation in your workplace that made you concerned about young children's safety? What did you do? How was the situation resolved?

8. Have you experienced a situation in your workplace in which your responsibilities to different stakeholders—such as the children, their families, your coworkers, your program's administration, or community agencies (for example, licensing, child protective services)—were in conflict? What did you do? How was the situation resolved?

9. What ethical issue have you encountered most frequently in your work? How have you addressed it?

10. Choose a dilemma you have faced in your work. Consider whether having the issue addressed in the program's staff or parent handbook might have helped avoid the dilemma. How might things have been different?

11. Consider an ethical dilemma you have faced in which you consulted the Code to help you resolve the situation. How was it helpful or not helpful to you?

12. If you had been the teacher involved in one of the case studies presented in this book, what might you have done differently in the situation? Why?

13. Have you ever encountered a situation in which a member of a child's family asked you to modify classroom activities that you believed to be beneficial? Under what circumstances might you be willing to exclude one child from a classroom activity at the family's request?

14. Imagine that you must inform a child's family member or a colleague of a resolution to a dilemma that goes against that person's wishes. Think of several ways you could diplomatically communicate your decision that would help preserve your relationship.

15. What have you learned from this book and your personal experiences about ethical decision making and using a professional code of ethics?

Glossary

best practices: teaching methods and techniques that, through experience and research, have proven to be effective

code of ethics: a document that defines the core values of a field and provides guidance for addressing conflicting obligations or responsibilities in the workplace

complex-client case: a situation that calls on professionals, including early childhood educators, to balance their obligations to a child with those they have to the child's family

cultural competence: the knowledge and skills needed to work effectively with children and families whose cultural backgrounds and experiences are different from one's own

ethical dilemma: a moral conflict that involves determining appropriate conduct when an individual faces conflicting professional values and responsibilities

ethical finesse: a creative response to an ethical dilemma that meets the needs of everyone involved and allows the teacher to avoid having to make a difficult decision

ethical issues: workplace situations that involve determining what is right and wrong, that concern rights and responsibilities, and that affect individuals' welfare

ethical responsibilities: behaviors that a professional must or must not engage in; spelled out in the NAEYC Code of Ethical Conduct

ethics: the study of right and wrong, duty, and obligation; it involves critical reflection on morality, the ability to examine the moral dimensions of relationships, and choosing between competing values

Ideals: descriptions of desirable, exemplary professional behavior

moral philosophy: the branch of philosophy concerned with the systematic study of morality

morality: what people view as good, right, or proper; their beliefs about their obligations; and their ideas about how they should behave

personal attributes: qualities or features regarded as characteristic or an inherent part of a person, including temperament (inborn ways of responding to situations) and dispositions (tendencies to respond to experiences in certain ways)

Principles (rules of professional conduct): rules that identify practices that are required, permitted, or prohibited; they help early childhood educators distinguish between acceptable and unacceptable professional behavior

profession: an occupation that involves having specialized knowledge, provides a service to society, and promotes a significant social value

professional: a person who carries out the work of a profession; requires specialized educational training, competence, and a commitment to the public good

professional core values: commitments held by a profession that are consciously and knowingly embraced by its practitioners because they contribute to society

professional ethics: the moral commitments of a profession that enhance practitioners' personal morality, concern actions of right and wrong in the workplace, and help individuals resolve moral dilemmas

resolution: a morally defensible course of action, reached through systematic analysis of an ethical dilemma

stakeholders: individuals who are involved in or affected by a course of action; in early childhood education, this can include children, families, employees, administrators, and the community

values: qualities or principles that individuals believe to be desirable or worthwhile and that they prize for themselves, for others, and for the world in which they live

References

Anderson, I. 2014. "Early Childhood Educators' Perception of Oregon's Professional Development System: A Hermeneutic Phenomenological Study." PhD diss., Portland State University. ProQuest (3669067).

Bassett, D.L. 2005. "Redefining the 'Public' Profession." *Rutgers Law Journal* 36 (3): 721–74.

CDSS (California Department of Social Services). 2011. "Frequently Asked Questions." *Child Abuse Mandated Reporter Training.* http://mandatedreporterca.com/faq/faq.htm.

Colker, L.J. 2008. "Twelve Characteristics of Effective Early Childhood Teachers." *Young Children* 63 (2): 68–73.

Cooper, D. 2003. *Ethics for Professionals in a Multicultural World.* Upper Saddle River, NJ: Pearson.

Derman-Sparks, L., & J.O. Edwards. 2010. *Anti-Bias Education for Young Children and Ourselves.* Washington, DC: NAEYC.

Driver, J. 2014. "The History of Utilitarianism." In *The Stanford Encyclopedia of Philosophy*, ed. E.N. Zalta. Stanford, CA: Stanford University. Last modified September 22. http://plato.stanford.edu/archives/win2014/entries/utilitarianism-history.

Feeney, S. 1987. "Ethical Case Studies for NAEYC Reader Response." *Young Children* 42 (4): 24–25.

Feeney, S. 1995. "Professionalism in Early Childhood Teacher Education." Focus on Ethics. *Journal of Early Childhood Teacher Education* 16 (3): 13–15.

Feeney, S. 2012. *Professionalism in Early Childhood Education: Doing Our Best for Young Children.* Englewood Cliffs, NJ: Pearson.

Feeney, S., & N.K. Freeman. 2011. "Misleading the State Inspector: The Response." Focus on Ethics. *Young Children* 66 (5): 68–70.

Feeney, S., & N.K. Freeman. 2012. "Messy Play: The Response." Focus on Ethics. *Young Children* 67 (2): 60–64.

Feeney, S., & N.K. Freeman. 2013. "The Birthday Cake: Balancing Responsibilities to Children and Families—The Response." *Young Children* 68 (1): 96–99.

Feeney, S., & N.K. Freeman. 2014a. "Reporting Classroom Behavior: Balancing Responsibilities to Children and Families—The Response." Focus on Ethics. *Young Children* 69 (4): 100–104.

Feeney, S., & N.K. Freeman. 2014b. "Standardized Testing in Kindergarten: The Response." Focus on Ethics. *Young Children* 69 (1): 84–88.

Feeney, S., & N.K. Freeman. 2015. "A Difficult Working Relationship: The Response." Focus on Ethics. *Young Children* 70 (4): 96–99.

Feeney, S., & N.K. Freeman. 2017. "'Don't Let My Son Dress Up as a Girl!'—The Response." Focus on Ethics. *Young Children* 72 (4): 90–93.

Feeney, S., N.K. Freeman, & E. Moravcik. 2016. *Teaching the NAEYC Code of Ethical Conduct: A Resource Guide.* Rev. ed. Washington, DC: NAEYC.

Feeney, S., L. Katz, & K. Kipnis. 1987. "Ethics Case Studies: The Working Mother." *Young Children* 43 (1): 16–19.

Feeney, S., & K. Kipnis. 1985. "Professional Ethics in Early Childhood Education." Public Policy Report and Survey. *Young Children* 40 (3): 54–58.

Feeney, S., E. Moravcik, & S. Nolte. 2016. *Who Am I in the Lives of Children? An Introduction to Early Childhood Education.* 10th ed. Englewood Cliffs, NJ: Pearson.

Fox, R.K. 2015. "Is He a Girl? Meeting the Needs of Children Who Are Gender Fluid." *Advances in Early Education and Day Care* 19: 161–76.

Freeman, N.K., & S. Feeney. 2016. "What Teachers Need to Know: Professional Ethics." Chap. 10 in *Handbook of Early Childhood Teacher Education*, eds. L.J. Couse & S.L Recchia, 148–162. New York: Routlege.

Frey, R.G. 2013. "Act-Utilitarianism." Chap. 10 in *The Blackwell Guide to Ethical Theory,* 2nd ed., eds. H. LaFollette & I. Persson, 221–37. Malden: MA: Wiley-Blackwell.

Gilliam, W.S., A.N. Maupin, C.R. Reyes, M. Accavitti, & F. Shic. 2016. "Do Early Educators' Implicit Biases Regarding Sex and Race Relate to Behavior Expectations and Recommendations of Preschool Expulsions and Suspensions?" Research study brief. New Haven, CT: Yale University Child Study Center. www.addressingracialmicroaggressions.com/wp-content/uploads/2016/10/Preschool-Implicit-Bias-Policy-Brief_final_9_26_276766_5379.pdf.

Gilligan, C. 1993. *In a Different Voice: Psychological Theory and Women's Development.* Rev. ed. Cambridge, MA: Harvard University Press.

Gonzalez-Mena, J. 2008. *Diversity in Early Care and Education: Honoring Differences.* 5th ed. New York: McGraw-Hill.

Harper Browne, C., C. Castro, & P. Lucier. 2016. "Honoring Parenting Values, Expectations, and Approaches Across Cultures." Chap. 3 in *Innovative Approaches to Supporting Families of Young Children,* eds. C.J. Shapiro & C. Harper Browne, 43–56. Cham, Switzerland: Springer International Publishing.

HHS (US Department of Health and Human Services) & ED (US Department of Education). 2014. "Policy Statement on Expulsion and Suspension Policies in Early Childhood Settings." Policy statement. www.acf .hhs.gov/sites/default/files/ecd/expulsion_suspension _final.pdf.

Hill, T.E. 2013. "Kantianism." Chap. 14 in *The Blackwell Guide to Ethical Theory,* 2nd ed., eds. H. LaFollette & I. Persson, 311–31. Malden, MA: Wiley-Blackwell.

Jaggar, A.M. 2013. "Feminist Ethics." Chap. 20 in *The Blackwell Guide to Ethical Theory,* 2nd ed., eds. H. LaFollette & I. Persson , 433–60. Malden, MA: Wiley-Blackwell.

Johnson, R., & A. Cureton. 2016. "Kant's Moral Philosophy." In *The Stanford Encyclopedia of Philosophy*, ed. E.N. Zalta. Stanford, CA: Stanford University. Last modified July 7. http://plato.stanford .edu/archives/fall2016/entries/kant-moral.

Katz, L.G., & E. Ward. [1978] 1991. *Ethical Behavior in Early Childhood Education.* Expanded ed. Washington, DC: NAEYC.

Kidder, R.M. 2009. *How Good People Make Tough Choices: Resolving the Dilemmas of Ethical Living.* Rev. ed. New York: Harper.

Kipnis, K. 1987. "How to Discuss Professional Ethics." *Young Children* 42 (4): 26–30.

Maxwell, B., & M. Schwimmer. 2016. "Seeking the Elusive Ethical Base of Teacher Professionalism in Canadian Codes of Ethics." *Teaching and Teacher Education* 59: 468–80.

Moran, G. l996. *A Grammar of Responsibility.* New York: Crossroad Press.

NAEYC. 1977. Minutes of the Governing Board Meeting. February.

NAEYC. 2004. "Code of Ethical Conduct: Supplement for Early Childhood Adult Educators." Washington, DC: NAEYC.

NAEYC. 2011. "Code of Ethical Conduct: Supplement for Early Childhood Program Administrators." Washington, DC: NAEYC.

NAEYC. 2016. *Code of Ethical Conduct and Statement of Commitment.* Brochure. Rev. ed. Washington, DC: NAEYC.

NAEYC. 2017. "About NAEYC." Accessed November 27. www.naeyc.org/about-us.

NAEYC & NAECS/SDE (National Association of Early Childhood Specialists in State Departments of Education). 2003. "Early Childhood Curriculum, Assessment, and Program Evaluation." Joint position statement. Washington, DC: NAEYC.

Noddings, N. 1984. *Caring: A Feminine Approach to Ethics and Morality.* Berkeley: University of California Press.

Osgood, J. 2010. "Reconstructing Professionalism in ECEC: The Case for the 'Critically Reflective Emotional Professional.'" *Early Years 30* (2): 119–33. doi:10.1080 /09575146.2010.490905.

Puckett, M.B., J.K. Black, D.S. Wittmer, & S.H. Peterson. 2008. *The Young Child: Development from Prebirth Through Age Eight.* 5th ed. Boston: Pearson.

Rhode, D.L., D. Luban, S.L. Cummings, & N.F. Engstrom. 2016. *Legal Ethics.* 7th ed. St. Paul, MN: Foundation Press.

Ryan, C., S.T. Russell, D. Huebner, R. Diaz, & J. Sanchez. 2010. "Family Acceptance in Adolescence and the Health of LGBT Young Adults." *Journal of Child and Adolescent Psychiatric Nursing* 23 (4): 205–13.

Schwimmer, M., & B. Maxwell, 2017. "Codes of Ethics and Teachers' Professional Autonomy." *Ethics and Education* 12 (2): 1–12.

Solomon, J. 2016. "Gender Identity and Expression in the Early Childhood Classroom: Influences on Development Within Sociocultural Contexts." *Voices of Practitioners: Teacher Research in Early Childhood Education* 11 (1): 61–79.

Staats, C., K. Capatosto, R.A. Wright, & D. Contractor. 2015. *State of the Science: Implicit Bias Review 2015.* Research report. Columbus, OH: Kirwan Institute for the Study of Race and Ethnicity. http://kirwaninstitute .osu.edu/wp-content/uploads/2015/05/2015-kirwan -implicit-bias.pdf.

Stonehouse, A. 1998. *Our Code of Ethics at Work.* Rev. ed. Vol. 5, No. 4 of *AECA Research in Practice Series.* Watson, ACT, Australia: Australian Early Childhood Association.

Tong, R., & N. Williams. 2009. "Feminist Ethics." In *The Stanford Encyclopedia of Philosophy*, ed. E.N. Zalta. Stanford, CA: Stanford University. Last modified May 4. http://plato.stanford.edu/archives/sum2016/entries /feminism-ethics.

Ungaretti, T., A.G. Dorsey, N.K. Freeman, & T.M. Bologna. 1997. "A Teacher Education Ethics Initiative: A Collaborative Response to a Professional Need." *Journal of Teacher Education* 48 (4): 271–80.

Appendix A: History and Development of the NAEYC Code of Ethical Conduct and Its Supplements

The NAEYC Governing Board first discussed creating a code of ethics for early childhood educators more than 40 years ago. Board members decided that it would be more feasible to develop a Statement of Commitment that all members could embrace in their efforts to "improve the quality of life for all children" (1977).

The subject of ethics was brought up again several years later, and the Governing Board decided to move forward with the development of a code of ethics. It identified three interrelated commitments that would guide this work:

- The association's code should be widely known and used. To achieve this goal, NAEYC believed that the Code needed to express deeply held beliefs about working with children and families and that members should view the Code as an essential part of their professional repertoire.
- The process of developing a code should involve as many of NAEYC's members as possible.
- The association should continue to systematically reflect on the ethical dimensions of working with young children even after a code had been adopted and was in use.

The process of developing a code of ethics for NAEYC began in 1984 with the publication of a survey in *Young Children*. The survey was designed to gauge members' interest in having a code of ethics and to identify some of the ethical issues they had encountered in their work with young children and families (Feeney & Kipnis 1985). Leaders in the code's development also conducted workshops in which participants worked to identify the field's core values and analyzed some of the ethical issues that had been shared by those who responded to the survey. The authors of the first version of the code relied on this input from NAEYC's members as well as their research on the codes of ethics in other fields to prepare a draft code to share with NAEYC's Governing Board.

The initial version of the NAEYC Code of Ethical Conduct was approved in 1989. Revisions designed to keep the Code current and to address emerging issues in the field were approved in 1992, 1997, and 2005.

In response to requests for ethical guidance from groups of early childhood professionals who have specialized roles, NAEYC developed two supplements to the Code. The Supplement for Adult Educators was developed collaboratively by the National Association of Early Childhood Teacher Educators (NAECTE), the Associate Degree Early Childhood Teacher Educators (ACCESS), and the Division of Early Childhood of the Council for Exceptional Children (DEC/CEC). It was approved by the NAEYC Governing Board in 2004 (Feeney 1995; NAEYC 2004; Ungaretti et al. 1997).

The Supplement for Early Childhood Program Administrators was developed with input from practitioners and the assistance of an advisory workgroup appointed by the NAEYC Board. It was approved by the Board in 2006 and was reaffirmed and updated in 2011 (NAEYC 2011).

Significant changes to the Code were made during the 2005 revision. They included the addition of a new Core Value: "To respect diversity in children, families, and colleagues." A number of items relating to the assessment of children were added in that revision, along with items that make a distinction between *individual* responsibilities to communities and society and the field's *collective* obligations to advocate for young children and their families.

The Code was reaffirmed and updated in 2011. This version is the one in use today, and is available as a brochure (NAEYC 2016). This update included changes to strengthen the ethical responsibilities of early childhood educators to families and the removal of the section on Responsibilities to Employees, as these ideals and principles were addressed by the Supplement for Early Childhood Program Administrators. This supplement was also updated and reaffirmed in 2011.

Appendix B: NAEYC Code of Ethical Conduct

Code of Ethical Conduct & Statement of Commitment

A position statement of the National Association for the Education of Young Children

Revised April 2005, Reaffirmed and Updated May 2011

Endorsed by the Association for Childhood Education International
Adopted by the National Association for Family Child Care

Preamble

NAEYC recognizes that those who work with young children face many daily decisions that have moral and ethical implications. The **NAEYC Code of Ethical Conduct** offers guidelines for responsible behavior and sets forth a common basis for resolving the principal ethical dilemmas encountered in early childhood care and education. **The Statement of Commitment** is not part of the Code but is a personal acknowledgement of an individual's willingness to embrace the distinctive values and moral obligations of the field of early childhood care and education.

The primary focus of the Code is on daily practice with children and their families in programs for children from birth through 8 years of age, such as infant/toddler programs, preschool and prekindergarten programs, child care centers, hospital and child life settings, family child care homes, kindergartens, and primary classrooms. When the issues involve young children, then these provisions also apply to specialists who do not work directly with children, including program administrators, parent educators, early childhood adult educators, and officials with responsibility for program monitoring and licensing. (*Note:* See also the "Code of Ethical Conduct: Supplement for Early Childhood Adult Educators" [available at NAEYC.org] and the "Code of Ethical Conduct: Supplement for Early Childhood Program Administrators" [on page 135 of this book and also available at NAEYC.org.])

The 2005 Revision and the 2011 Reaffirmation and Updating of the Code of Ethical Conduct

NAEYC's Code of Ethical Conduct is reviewed periodically for possible revision. When the Governing Board of NAEYC determines that a full revision of the Code is necessary, the Association's process for position statement development and revision begins. This process involves extensive input and review by NAEYC membership, other early childhood education specialists, and, when appropriate, individuals with expertise in the area addressed by the position statement. Such was the case for the 2005 revision, in which a new Core Value, nine new Ideals, and fourteen new Principles were added to the Code—focused primarily on respect for diversity and concerns regarding accountability and child assessments.

In 2011, the Governing Board reaffirmed the 2005 Code and updated this position statement to reflect consistency with the "Supplement for Early Childhood Program Administrators." Specifically, Section III-C (Ethical Responsibilities to Colleagues/Responsibilities to Employees) was deleted, as these Ideals and Principles are addressed in the Supplement. Other minor modifications were also made to ensure clarity and consistency. In addition, changes were made to Ideals and Principles that regard responsibilities to families to ensure alignment with current family engagement best practices in the field.

Core Values

Standards of ethical behavior in early childhood care and education are based on commitment to the following core values that are deeply rooted in the history of the field of early childhood care and education. We have made a commitment to

- Appreciate childhood as a unique and valuable stage of the human life cycle
- Base our work on knowledge of how children develop and learn
- Appreciate and support the bond between the child and family
- Recognize that children are best understood and supported in the context of family, culture,* community, and society
- Respect the dignity, worth, and uniqueness of each individual (child, family member, and colleague)
- Respect diversity in children, families, and colleagues
- Recognize that children and adults achieve their full potential in the context of relationships that are based on trust and respect

Conceptual Framework

The Code sets forth a framework of professional responsibilities in four sections. Each section addresses an area of professional relationships: (1) with children, (2) with families, (3) among colleagues, and (4) with the community and society. Each section includes an introduction to the primary responsibilities of the early childhood practitioner in that context. The introduction is followed by a set of ideals (I) that reflect exemplary professional practice and by a set of principles (P)

describing practices that are required, prohibited, or permitted.

The **ideals** reflect the aspirations of practitioners. The **principles** guide conduct and assist practitioners in resolving ethical dilemmas.** Both ideals and principles are intended to direct practitioners to those questions which, when responsibly answered, can provide the basis for conscientious decision making. While the Code provides specific direction for addressing some ethical dilemmas, many others will require the practitioner to combine the guidance of the Code with professional judgment.

The ideals and principles in this Code present a shared framework of professional responsibility that affirms our commitment to the core values of our field. The Code publicly acknowledges the responsibilities that we in the field have assumed, and in so doing supports ethical behavior in our work. Practitioners who face situations with ethical dimensions are urged to seek guidance in the applicable parts of this Code and in the spirit that informs the whole.

Often "the right answer"—the best ethical course of action to take—is not obvious. There may be no readily apparent, positive way to handle a situation. When one important value contradicts another, we face an ethical dilemma. When we face a dilemma, it is our professional responsibility to consult the Code and all relevant parties to find the most ethical resolution.

Section I:

Ethical Responsibilities to Children

Childhood is a unique and valuable stage in the human life cycle. Our paramount responsibility is to provide care and education in settings that are safe, healthy, nurturing, and responsive for each child. We are committed to supporting children's development and learning; respecting individual differences; and helping children learn to live, play, and work cooperatively. We are also committed to promoting children's self-awareness, competence, self-worth, resiliency, and physical well-being.

---

*Culture includes ethnicity, racial identity, economic level, family structure, language, and religious and political beliefs, which profoundly influence each child's development and relationship to the world.

**There is not necessarily a corresponding principle for each ideal.

Ideals

I-1.1—To be familiar with the knowledge base of early childhood care and education and to stay informed through continuing education and training.

I-1.2—To base program practices upon current knowledge and research in the field of early childhood education, child development, and related disciplines, as well as on particular knowledge of each child.

I-1.3—To recognize and respect the unique qualities, abilities, and potential of each child.

I-1.4—To appreciate the vulnerability of children and their dependence on adults.

I-1.5—To create and maintain safe and healthy settings that foster children's social, emotional, cognitive, and physical development and that respect their dignity and their contributions.

I-1.6—To use assessment instruments and strategies that are appropriate for the children to be assessed, that are used only for the purposes for which they were designed, and that have the potential to benefit children.

I-1.7—To use assessment information to understand and support children's development and learning, to support instruction, and to identify children who may need additional services.

I-1.8—To support the right of each child to play and learn in an inclusive environment that meets the needs of children with and without disabilities.

I-1.9—To advocate for and ensure that all children, including those with special needs, have access to the support services needed to be successful.

I-1.10—To ensure that each child's culture, language, ethnicity, and family structure are recognized and valued in the program.

I-1.11—To provide all children with experiences in a language that they know, as well as support children in maintaining the use of their home language and in learning English.

I-1.12—To work with families to provide a safe and smooth transition as children and families move from one program to the next.

Principles

P-1.1—**Above all, we shall not harm children. We shall not participate in practices that are emotionally damaging, physically harmful, disrespectful, degrading, dangerous, exploitative, or intimidating to children.** *This principle has precedence over all others in this Code.*

P-1.2—We shall care for and educate children in positive emotional and social environments that are cognitively stimulating and that support each child's culture, language, ethnicity, and family structure.

P-1.3—We shall not participate in practices that discriminate against children by denying benefits, giving special advantages, or excluding them from programs or activities on the basis of their sex, race, national origin, immigration status, preferred home language, religious beliefs, medical condition, disability, or the marital status/family structure, sexual orientation, or religious beliefs or other affiliations of their families. (Aspects of this principle do not apply in programs that have a lawful mandate to provide services to a particular population of children.)

P-1.4—We shall use two-way communications to involve all those with relevant knowledge (including families and staff) in decisions concerning a child, as appropriate, ensuring confidentiality of sensitive information. (See also P-2.4.)

P-1.5—We shall use appropriate assessment systems, which include multiple sources of information, to provide information on children's learning and development.

P-1.6—We shall strive to ensure that decisions such as those related to enrollment, retention, or assignment to special education services, will be based on multiple sources of information and will never be based on a single assessment, such as a test score or a single observation.

P-1.7—We shall strive to build individual relationships with each child; make individualized adaptations in teaching strategies, learning environments, and curricula; and consult with the family so that each child benefits from the program. If after such efforts have been exhausted, the current placement does not meet a child's needs, or the child is seriously jeopardizing the ability of other children to benefit from the program, we shall collaborate with the child's family and appropriate specialists to determine the additional services needed and/or the placement option(s) most likely to ensure the child's success. (Aspects of this principle may not apply in programs that have a lawful mandate to provide services to a particular population of children.)

P-1.8—We shall be familiar with the risk factors for and symptoms of child abuse and neglect, including physical, sexual, verbal, and emotional abuse and physical, emotional, educational, and medical neglect. We shall know and follow state laws and community procedures that protect children against abuse and neglect.

P-1.9—When we have reasonable cause to suspect child abuse or neglect, we shall report it to the appropriate community agency and follow up to ensure that appropriate action has been taken. When appropriate, parents or guardians will be informed that the referral will be or has been made.

P-1.10—When another person tells us of his or her suspicion that a child is being abused or neglected, we shall assist that person in taking appropriate action in order to protect the child.

P-1.11—When we become aware of a practice or situation that endangers the health, safety, or well-being of children, we have an ethical responsibility to protect children or inform parents and/or others who can.

Section II:

Ethical Responsibilities to Families

Families* are of primary importance in children's development. Because the family and the early childhood practitioner have a common interest in the child's well-being, we acknowledge a primary responsibility to bring about communication, cooperation, and collaboration between the home and early childhood program in ways that enhance the child's development.

*The term *family* may include those adults, besides parents, with the responsibility of being involved in educating, nurturing, and advocating for the child.

Ideals

I-2.1—To be familiar with the knowledge base related to working effectively with families and to stay informed through continuing education and training.

I-2.2—To develop relationships of mutual trust and create partnerships with the families we serve.

I-2.3—To welcome all family members and encourage them to participate in the program, including involvement in shared decision making.

I-2.4—To listen to families, acknowledge and build upon their strengths and competencies, and learn from families as we support them in their task of nurturing children.

I-2.5—To respect the dignity and preferences of each family and to make an effort to learn about its structure, culture, language, customs, and beliefs to ensure a culturally consistent environment for all children and families.

I-2.6—To acknowledge families' childrearing values and their right to make decisions for their children.

I-2.7—To share information about each child's education and development with families and to help them understand and appreciate the current knowledge base of the early childhood profession.

I-2.8—To help family members enhance their understanding of their children, as staff are enhancing their understanding of each child through communications with families, and support family members in the continuing development of their skills as parents.

I-2.9—To foster families' efforts to build support networks and, when needed, participate in building networks for families by providing them with opportunities to interact with program staff, other families, community resources, and professional services.

Principles

P-2.1—We shall not deny family members access to their child's classroom or program setting unless access is denied by court order or other legal restriction.

P-2.2—We shall inform families of program philosophy, policies, curriculum, assessment system, cultural practices, and personnel qualifications, and explain why we teach as we do—which should be in accordance with our ethical responsibilities to children (see Section I).

P-2.3—We shall inform families of and, when appropriate, involve them in policy decisions. (See also I-2.3.)

P-2.4—We shall ensure that the family is involved in significant decisions affecting their child. (See also P-1.4.)

P-2.5—We shall make every effort to communicate effectively with all families in a language that they understand. We shall use community resources for translation and interpretation when we do not have sufficient resources in our own programs.

P-2.6—As families share information with us about their children and families, we shall ensure that families' input is an important contribution to the planning and implementation of the program.

P-2.7—We shall inform families about the nature and purpose of the program's child assessments and how data about their child will be used.

P-2.8—We shall treat child assessment information confidentially and share this information only when there is a legitimate need for it.

P-2.9—We shall inform the family of injuries and incidents involving their child, of risks such as exposures to communicable diseases that might result in infection, and of occurrences that might result in emotional stress.

P-2.10—Families shall be fully informed of any proposed research projects involving their children and shall have the opportunity to give or withhold consent without penalty. We shall not permit or participate in research that could in any way hinder the education, development, or well-being of children.

P-2.11—We shall not engage in or support exploitation of families. We shall not use our relationship with a family for private advantage or personal gain, or enter into relationships with family members that might impair our effectiveness working with their children.

P-2.12—We shall develop written policies for the protection of confidentiality and the disclosure of children's records. These policy documents shall be made available to all program personnel and families. Disclosure of children's records beyond family members, program personnel, and consultants having an obligation of confidentiality shall require familial consent (except in cases of abuse or neglect).

P-2.13—We shall maintain confidentiality and shall respect the family's right to privacy, refraining from disclosure of confidential information and intrusion into family life. However, when we have reason to believe that a child's welfare is at risk, it is permissible to share confidential information with agencies, as well as with individuals who have legal responsibility for intervening in the child's interest.

P-2.14—In cases where family members are in conflict with one another, we shall work openly, sharing our observations of the child, to help all parties involved make informed decisions. We shall refrain from becoming an advocate for one party.

P-2.15—We shall be familiar with and appropriately refer families to community resources and professional support services. After a referral has been made, we shall follow up to ensure that services have been appropriately provided.

Section III:

Ethical Responsibilities to Colleagues

In a caring, cooperative workplace, human dignity is respected, professional satisfaction is promoted, and positive relationships are developed and sustained. Based upon our core values, our primary responsibility to colleagues is to establish and maintain settings and relationships that support productive work and meet professional needs. The same ideals that apply to children also apply as we interact with adults in the workplace. (Note: Section III includes responsibilities to coworkers and to employers. See the "Code of Ethical Conduct: Supplement for Early Childhood Program Administrators" for responsibilities to personnel [*employees* in the original 2005 Code revision].

A—Responsibilities to coworkers

Ideals

I-3A.1—To establish and maintain relationships of respect, trust, confidentiality, collaboration, and cooperation with coworkers.

I-3A.2—To share resources with coworkers, collaborating to ensure that the best possible early childhood care and education program is provided.

I-3A.3—To support coworkers in meeting their professional needs and in their professional development.

I-3A.4—To accord coworkers due recognition of professional achievement.

Principles

P-3A.1—We shall recognize the contributions of colleagues to our program and not participate in practices that diminish their reputations or impair their effectiveness in working with children and families.

P-3A.2—When we have concerns about the professional behavior of a coworker, we shall first let that person know of our concern in a way that shows respect for personal dignity and for the diversity to be found among staff members, and then attempt to resolve the matter collegially and in a confidential manner.

P-3A.3—We shall exercise care in expressing views regarding the personal attributes or professional conduct of coworkers. Statements should be based on firsthand knowledge, not hearsay, and relevant to the interests of children and programs.

P-3A.4—We shall not participate in practices that discriminate against a coworker because of sex, race, national origin, religious beliefs or other affiliations, age, marital status/family structure, disability, or sexual orientation.

B—Responsibilities to employers

Ideals

I-3B.1—To assist the program in providing the highest quality of service.

I-3B.2—To do nothing that diminishes the reputation of the program in which we work unless it is violating laws and regulations designed to protect children or is violating the provisions of this Code.

Principles

P-3B.1—We shall follow all program policies. When we do not agree with program policies, we shall attempt to effect change through constructive action within the organization.

P-3B.2—We shall speak or act on behalf of an organization only when authorized. We shall take care to acknowledge when we are speaking for the organization and when we are expressing a personal judgment.

P-3B.3—We shall not violate laws or regulations designed to protect children and shall take appropriate action consistent with this Code when aware of such violations.

P-3B.4—If we have concerns about a colleague's behavior, and children's well-being is not at risk, we may address the concern with that individual. If children are at risk or the situation does not improve after it has been brought to the colleague's attention, we shall report the colleague's unethical or incompetent behavior to an appropriate authority.

P-3B.5—When we have a concern about circumstances or conditions that impact the quality of care and education within the program, we shall inform the program's administration or, when necessary, other appropriate authorities.

Section IV:

Ethical Responsibilities to Community and Society

Early childhood programs operate within the context of their immediate community made up of families and other institutions concerned with children's welfare. Our responsibilities to the community are to provide programs that meet the diverse needs of families, to cooperate with agencies and professions that share the responsibility for children, to assist families in gaining access to those agencies and allied professionals, and to assist in the development of community programs that are needed but not currently available.

As individuals, we acknowledge our responsibility to provide the best possible programs of care and education for children and to conduct ourselves with honesty and integrity. Because of our specialized expertise in early childhood development and education and because the larger society shares responsibility for the welfare and protection of young children, we acknowledge a collective obligation to advocate for the best interests of children within early childhood programs and in the larger community and to serve as a voice for young children everywhere.

The ideals and principles in this section are presented to distinguish between those that pertain to the work of the individual early childhood educator and those that more typically are engaged in collectively on behalf of the best interests of children—with the understanding that individual early childhood educators have a shared responsibility for addressing the ideals and principles that are identified as "collective."

Ideal (Individual)

1-4.1—To provide the community with high-quality early childhood care and education programs and services.

Ideals (Collective)

I-4.2—To promote cooperation among professionals and agencies and interdisciplinary collaboration among professions concerned with addressing issues in the health, education, and well-being of young children, their families, and their early childhood educators.

I-4.3—To work through education, research, and advocacy toward an environmentally safe world in which all children receive health care, food, and shelter; are nurtured; and live free from violence in their home and their communities.

I-4.4—To work through education, research, and advocacy toward a society in which all young children have access to high-quality early care and education programs.

I-4.5—To work to ensure that appropriate assessment systems, which include multiple sources of information, are used for purposes that benefit children.

I-4.6—To promote knowledge and understanding of young children and their needs. To work toward greater societal acknowledgment of children's rights and greater social acceptance of responsibility for the well-being of all children.

I-4.7—To support policies and laws that promote the well-being of children and families, and to work to change those that impair their well-being. To participate in developing policies and laws that are needed, and to cooperate with families and other individuals and groups in these efforts.

I-4.8—To further the professional development of the field of early childhood care and education and to strengthen its commitment to realizing its core values as reflected in this Code.

Principles (Individual)

P-4.1—We shall communicate openly and truthfully about the nature and extent of services that we provide.

P-4.2—We shall apply for, accept, and work in positions for which we are personally well-suited and professionally qualified. We shall not offer services that we do not have the competence, qualifications, or resources to provide.

P-4.3—We shall carefully check references and shall not hire or recommend for employment any person whose competence, qualifications, or character makes him or her unsuited for the position.

P-4.4—We shall be objective and accurate in reporting the knowledge upon which we base our program practices.

P-4.5—We shall be knowledgeable about the appropriate use of assessment strategies and instruments and interpret results accurately to families.

P-4.6—We shall be familiar with laws and regulations that serve to protect the children in our programs and be vigilant in ensuring that these laws and regulations are followed.

P-4.7—When we become aware of a practice or situation that endangers the health, safety, or well-being of children, we have an ethical responsibility to protect children or inform parents and/or others who can.

P-4.8—We shall not participate in practices that are in violation of laws and regulations that protect the children in our programs.

P-4.9—When we have evidence that an early childhood program is violating laws or regulations protecting children, we shall report the violation to appropriate authorities who can be expected to remedy the situation.

P-4.10—When a program violates or requires its employees to violate this Code, it is permissible, after fair assessment of the evidence, to disclose the identity of that program.

Principles (Collective)

P-4.11—When policies are enacted for purposes that do not benefit children, we have a collective responsibility to work to change these policies.

P-4.12—When we have evidence that an agency that provides services intended to ensure children's well-being is failing to meet its obligations, we acknowledge a collective ethical responsibility to report the problem to appropriate authorities or to the public. We shall be vigilant in our follow-up until the situation is resolved.

P-4.13—When a child protection agency fails to provide adequate protection for abused or neglected children, we acknowledge a collective ethical responsibility to work toward the improvement of these services.

Statement of Commitment*

As an individual who works with young children, I commit myself to furthering the values of early childhood education as they are reflected in the ideals and principles of the NAEYC Code of Ethical Conduct. To the best of my ability I will

- Never harm children.
- Ensure that programs for young children are based on current knowledge and research of child development and early childhood education.
- Respect and support families in their task of nurturing children.
- Respect colleagues in early childhood care and education and support them in maintaining the NAEYC Code of Ethical Conduct.
- Serve as an advocate for children, their families, and their teachers in community and society.
- Stay informed of and maintain high standards of professional conduct.
- Engage in an ongoing process of self-reflection, realizing that personal characteristics, biases, and beliefs have an impact on children and families.
- Be open to new ideas and be willing to learn from the suggestions of others.
- Continue to learn, grow, and contribute as a professional.
- Honor the ideals and principles of the NAEYC Code of Ethical Conduct.

*This Statement of Commitment is not part of the Code but is a personal acknowledgement of the individual's willingness to embrace the distinctive values and moral obligations of the field of early childhood care and education. It is recognition of the moral obligations that lead to an individual becoming part of the profession.

Appendix C: Code of Ethical Conduct—Supplement for Early Childhood Program Administrators

Code of Ethical Conduct
Supplement for Early Childhood Program Administrators

A position statement supplement of the National Association
for the Education of Young Children

Adopted July 2006, Reaffirmed and Updated May 2011

Adopted by the National Association for Family Child Care

Administrators of programs for young children are responsible for overseeing all program operations, serving as leaders in their programs, and representing the field to the community. Early childhood program administrators are called upon to sustain relationships with a wide variety of clients. They interact with and have responsi bilities to children, families, program personnel, governing boards and sponsoring agencies, funders, regulatory agencies, their community, and the profession.

Program administrators deal with unique responsibilities and ethical challenges in the course of managing and guiding their programs and assume leadership roles within and beyond their programs. As managers and leaders, they are called upon to share their professional knowledge and expertise with families, personnel, governing boards, and others; demonstrate empathy for the families and children they serve; and communicate respect for the skills, knowledge, and expertise of teaching staff, other personnel, and families. Administrators accept primary responsibility for executing the program's mission as well as developing and carrying out program policies and procedures that support that mission. They also make a commitment to continue their own professional development and the continuing education of the personnel in the program they lead. Administrators also may be advocates for all children being able to gain access to quality programming. Some of the challenges faced by administrators involve balancing their obligations to support and nurture children with their responsibility to address the needs and safeguard the rights of families and personnel and respond to the requirements of their boards and sponsoring agencies.

Purpose of the Supplement

Like those in the field who work directly with young children, program administrators are regularly called upon to make decisions of a moral and ethical nature. The NAEYC Code of Ethical Conduct (revised 2005, reaffirmed and updated 2011) is a foundational document that maps the ethical dimensions of early childhood educators' work in early care and education programs. Program administrators share the ethical obligations assumed by all early childhood educators— obligations that are reflected in the core values, ideals, and principles set forth in the Code. Administrators embrace the central commitment of the early care and education field—and the Code—to ensure the well-being and support the healthy development of young children.

Given the nature of their responsibilities, however, administrators face some additional ethical challenges. Conflicts often surface in the areas of enrollment policies; dealings with personnel; and relationships with families, licensors, governing boards, sponsoring agencies, and others in the community. The existing Code is a valuable resource that addresses many of the ethical issues encountered by administrators. However, it does not provide all of the guidance that they need to address the unique ethical issues that arise in their work. This Supplement offers additional core values, ideals, and principles related to the frequently recurring ethical issues encountered by administrators.

Core Values

In addition to the core values spelled out in the NAEYC Code of Ethical Conduct, early childhood program administrators commit themselves to the following additional core values.

We make a commitment to

- Recognize that we have many responsibilities—to children, families, personnel, governing boards, sponsoring agencies, funders, regulatory agencies, the community, and the profession—and that the well-being of the children in our care is our primary responsibility, above our obligations to other constituencies.

- Recognize the importance of and maintain a humane and fulfilling work environment for personnel and volunteers.

- Be committed to the professional development of staff.

Conceptual Framework

This document sets forth a conception of early childhood program administrators' professional responsibilities in five areas, some of which differ from those identified in the NAEYC Code. Each section addresses an area of professional relationships: (1) with children, (2) with families, (3) with personnel, (4) with sponsoring agencies and governing boards, and (5) with the community and society. The items in each section address the unique ethical responsibilities of administrators in early care and education settings.

Definitions

Administrator

The individual responsible for planning, implementing, and evaluating a child care, preschool, kindergarten, or primary grade program. The administrator's title may vary, depending on the program type or sponsorship of the program. Common titles include director, site manager, administrator, program manager, early childhood coordinator, and principal.

(*Note:* The definition of *administrator* and other relevant text in this Supplement are consistent with the Leadership and Management standard of the NAEYC Early Childhood Program Standards and Accreditation Criteria.)

Personnel

Staff members employed, directed, or supervised by an administrator. Here, unless otherwise noted, *personnel* includes all program staff and volunteers providing services to children and/or families. (*Note:* Because program administrators may be supervisors and not employers, we have adopted the terms *personnel* and *staff* in lieu of *employees* for this Supplement to the Code.)

Ideals and Principles

This Supplement identifies additional *ideals* that reflect exemplary practice (our aspirations) and *principles* describing practices that are required, prohibited, or permitted. The principles guide conduct and assist practitioners in resolving ethical dilemmas. Together, the ideals and principles are intended to direct practitioners to questions that, when responsibly answered, provide the basis for conscientious decision making. While the Code and this Supplement provide specific direction for addressing some ethical dilemmas, many others will require early childhood program administrators to combine the guidance of the Code and/or this Supplement with their best professional judgment.

The ideals and principles in the Code and this Supplement present a shared framework of professional responsibility that affirms our commitment to the core values of our field. The Code and the Supplement publicly acknowledge the responsibilities that early childhood professionals assume and, in so doing, support ethical behavior in our work. Practitioners who face situations with ethical dimensions are urged to seek guidance in the applicable parts of the Code/Supplement and in the spirit that informs the whole.

The ideals and principles in this Supplement are based on early childhood program administrators' descriptions of ethical dilemmas they have encountered in their work. They are designed to inspire and guide administrators toward actions that reflect the field's current understanding of ethical responsibility.

The Supplement also includes items from the NAEYC Code that directly relate to the work of administrators—some are duplicates of Code ideals or principles, and some are adaptations. Items from the Code that are repeated or adapted for this Supplement are cross-referenced with their corresponding ideals and principles, with the Code references indicated in parentheses. Other items that expand and extend the NAEYC Code were written specifically for this Supplement. (*Note:* There is not necessarily a corresponding principle for each ideal.)

1. Ethical Responsibilities to Children

The early childhood program administrator's paramount responsibility is to ensure that programs for children provide settings that are safe, healthy, nurturing, and responsive for each child. Administrators are committed to establishing and maintaining programs that support children's development and learning; promote respect for individual differences; and help children learn to live, play, and work cooperatively. Administrators are also committed to ensuring that the program promotes children's self-awareness, competence, self-worth, resiliency, and physical well-being.

Ideals

I-1.1 To ensure that children's needs are the first priority in administrative decision making, recognizing that a child's well-being cannot be separated from that of his/her family.

I-1.2 To provide a high-quality program based on current knowledge of child development and best practices in early care and education.

Principles

P-1.1 We shall place the welfare and safety of children above other obligations (for example, to families, program personnel, employing agency, community). *This item takes precedence over all others in this Supplement.*

P-1.2 We shall ensure that the programs we administer are safe and developmentally appropriate in accordance with standards of the field, including those developed and endorsed by NAEYC and other professional associations.

P-1.3 We shall have clearly stated policies for the respectful treatment of children and adults in all contacts made by staff, parents, volunteers, student teachers, and other adults. We shall appropriately address incidents that are not consistent with our policies.

P-1.4 We shall support children's well-being by encouraging the development of strong bonds between children and their families and between children and their teachers.

P-1.5 We shall support children's well-being by promoting connections with their culture and collaborating with communities to ensure cultural consistency between the program and families' childrearing practices.

P-1.6 We shall make every effort to provide the necessary resources (staff, consultation, other human resources, equipment, and so on) to ensure that all children, including those with special needs, can benefit from the program.

P-1.7 We shall ensure that there is a plan for appropriate transitions for children when they enter our program, move from one classroom to another within our program, and when they leave.

P-1.8 We shall apply all policies regarding our obligations to children consistently and fairly.

P-1.9 We shall review all program policies set forth by sponsoring agencies and governing bodies to ensure that they are in the best interest of the children.

P-1.10 We shall express our professional concerns about directives from the sponsoring agency or governing body when we believe that a mandated practice is not in the best interest of children.

P-1.11 If we determine that a policy does not benefit children, we shall work to change it. If we determine that a program policy is harmful to children, we shall suspend its implementation while working to honor the intent of the policy in ways that are not harmful to children.

2. Ethical Responsibilities to Families

The administrator sets the tone for the program in establishing and supporting an understanding of the family's role in their children's development. Administrators strive to promote communication, cooperation, and collaboration between the home and the program in ways that enhance each child's development. Because administrators provide the link between the family and direct services for children, they often encounter ethical issues in this area of responsibility.

Ideals

I-2.1 To design programs and policies inclusive of and responsive to diverse families.

I-2.2 To serve as a resource for families by providing information and referrals to services in the larger community.

I-2.3 To advocate for the needs and rights of families in the program and the larger community.

I-2.4 To support families in their role as advocate for their children and themselves.

I-2.5 To create and maintain a climate of trust and candor that fosters two-way communication and enables parents/guardians to speak and act in the best interest of their children.

Principles

P-2.1 We shall work to create a respectful environment for and a working relationship with all families, regardless of family members' sex, race, national origin, immigration status, preferred home language, religious belief or affiliation, age, marital status/family structure, disability, or sexual orientation.

P-2.2 We shall provide families with complete and honest information concerning program philosophy, educational practices, and the services provided.

P-2.3 We shall make every attempt to use two-way communication to convey information in ways that are accessible by every family served.

P-2.4 We shall establish clear operating policies and make them available to families in advance of their child entering the program.

P-2.5 We shall develop enrollment policies that clearly describe admission policies and priorities.

P-2.6 We shall develop policies that clearly state the circumstances under which a child or family may be asked to leave the program. We shall refuse to provide services for children only if the program will not benefit them or if their presence jeopardizes the ability of other children to benefit from the program or prevents personnel from doing their jobs.

P-2.7 We shall assist families in finding appropriate alternatives when we believe their children cannot benefit from the program or when their presence jeopardizes the ability of other children to benefit from the program or prevents personnel from doing their jobs.

P-2.8 We shall apply all policies regarding obligations to families consistently and fairly.

P-2.9 In decisions concerning children and programs, we shall draw upon our relationships with families as well as each family's knowledge of their child. (See also P-3.7 in this Supplement.)

P-2.10 We shall respond to families' requests to the extent that the requests are congruent with program philosophy, standards of good practice, and the resources of the program. We shall not honor any request that puts a child in a situation that would create physical or emotional harm. In such instances, we shall communicate with the family the reason(s) why the request was not honored and work toward an alternative solution.

P-2.11 We shall work to achieve shared understanding between families and staff members. In disagreements, we shall help all parties express their particular needs and perspectives. (*Note:* This is repeated in Section 3 [P-3.16] to emphasize the responsibility to both staff and family members.)

3. Ethical Responsibilities to Personnel

Early childhood program administrators are managers with the responsibility for providing oversight for all program operations, as well as serving as leaders in early care and education programs. They are responsible for creating and maintaining a caring, cooperative workplace that respects human dignity, promotes professional satisfaction, and models positive relationships. Administrators must exemplify the highest possible standards of professional practice both within and beyond the program. Ethical responsibilities to personnel include those that are related to working with staff they supervise and/or employ as well as the unions or groups that represent these staff. (*Note:* Administrators' ethical responsibilities to coworkers and employers are included in the Code of Ethical Conduct, Section III, Part A and Part B.)

Ideals

I-3.1 To create and promote policies and working conditions that are physically and emotionally safe and foster mutual respect, cooperation, collaboration, competence, well-being, confidentiality, and self-esteem.

I-3.2 To create and maintain a climate of trust and candor that enables staff to speak and act in the best interest of children, families, and the field of early care and education.

I-3.3 To coach and mentor staff, helping them realize their potential within the field of early care and education.

I-3.4 To strive to secure adequate and equitable compensation (salary and benefits) for those who work with or on behalf of young children.

I-3.5 To encourage and support continual development of staff in becoming more skilled and knowledgeable practitioners.

Principles

P-3.1 We shall provide staff members with safe and supportive working conditions that respect human dignity, honor confidences, and permit them to carry out their responsibilities through performance evaluation, written grievance procedures, constructive feedback, and opportunities for continuing professional development and advancement.

P-3.2 We shall develop and maintain comprehensive written personnel policies that define program standards. These policies shall be given to new staff members and shall be easily accessible and available for review by all staff members.

P-3.3 We shall apply all policies regarding our work with personnel consistently and fairly.

P-3.4 We shall be familiar with and abide by the rules and regulations developed by unions or other groups representing the interests or rights of personnel in our programs.

P-3.5 We shall support and encourage personnel in their efforts to implement programming that enhances the development and learning of the children served.

P-3.6 We shall act immediately to prevent staff from implementing activities or practices that put any child in a situation that creates physical or emotional harm.

P-3.7 In decisions concerning children and programs, we shall draw upon the education, training, experience, and expertise of staff members. (See also P-2.9 in this Supplement.)

P-3.8 We shall work to ensure that ongoing training is available and accessible, represents current understandings of best practice, and is relevant to staff members' responsibilities.

P-3.9 We shall inform staff whose performance does not meet program expectations of areas of concern and, when possible, assist in improving their performance.

P-3.10 We shall provide guidance, additional professional development, and coaching for staff whose practices are not appropriate. In instances in which a staff member cannot satisfy reasonable expectations for practice, we shall counsel the staff member to pursue a more appropriate position.

P-3.11 We shall conduct personnel dismissals, when necessary, in accordance with all applicable laws and regulations. We shall inform staff who are dismissed of the reasons for termination. When a dismissal is for cause, justification must be based on evidence of inadequate or inappropriate behavior that is accurately documented, current, and available for the staff member to review.

P-3.12 In making personnel evaluations and recommendations, we shall make judgments based on fact and relevant to the interests of children and programs.

P-3.13 We shall make hiring, retention, termination, and promotion decisions based solely on a person's competence, record of accomplishment, ability to carry out the responsibilities of the position, and professional preparation specific to the developmental levels of children in his/her care.

P-3.14 We shall not make hiring, retention, termination, and promotion decisions based on an individual's sex, race, national origin, religious beliefs or other affiliations, age, marital status/family structure, disability, or sexual orientation. We shall be familiar with and observe laws and regulations that pertain to employment discrimination. (Aspects of this principle do not apply to programs that have a lawful mandate to determine eligibility based on one or more of the criteria identified above.)

P-3.15 We shall maintain confidentiality in dealing with issues related to an employee's job performance and shall respect an employee's right to privacy regarding personal issues.

P-3.16 We shall work to achieve shared understandings between families and staff members. In disagreements, we shall help all parties express their particular needs and perspectives. (*Note:* This is repeated from Section 2 [P-2.11] to emphasize the responsibility to both staff and family members.)

4. Ethical Responsibilities to Sponsoring Agencies and Governing Bodies

Programs providing early care and education operate under a variety of public and private auspices with diverse governing structures and missions. All early childhood program administrators are responsible to their governing and funding bodies. Administrators ensure the program's stability and reputation by recruiting, selecting, orienting, and supervising personnel; following sound fiscal practices; and securing and maintaining licensure and accreditation. Administrators are also responsible for overseeing day-to-day program operations and fostering positive relationships among children, families, staff, and the community.

Administrators' responsibilities to sponsoring agencies and governing bodies are optimally met in a collaborative manner. Administrators establish and maintain partnerships with sponsoring agency representatives, board members, and other stakeholders to design and improve services for children and their families.

Ideals

I–4.1 To ensure to the best of our ability that the program pursues its stated mission.

I-4.2 To provide program leadership that reflects best practices in early care and education and program administration.

I-4.3 To plan and institute ongoing program improvements.

I-4.4 To be ambassadors within the community, creating goodwill for program sponsors as well as for the program itself.

I-4.5 To advocate on behalf of children and families in interactions with sponsoring agency staff and governing body members for high-quality early care and educa tion programs and services for children.

Principles

P-4.1 We shall ensure compliance with all relevant regulations and standards.

P-4.2 We shall do our jobs conscientiously, attending to all areas that fall within the scope of our responsibility.

P-4.3 We shall manage resources responsibly and accurately account for their use.

P-4.4 To ensure that the program's sponsoring agency and governing body are prepared to make wise decisions, we shall thoroughly and honestly communicate necessary information.

P-4.5 We shall evaluate our programs using agreed upon standards and report our findings to the appropriate authority.

P-4.6 In presenting information to governing bodies we shall make every effort to preserve confidentiality regarding children, families, and staff unless there is a compelling reason for divulging the information.

5. Ethical Responsibilities to Community, Society, and the Field of Early Childhood Education

Like those of all early childhood educators, administrators' responsibilities to the community include cooperating with agencies and professionals that share the responsibility for children, supporting families in gaining access to services provided by those agencies and professionals, and assisting in the development of community programs and services.

Early childhood program administrators often have the knowledge, expertise, and education to assume leadership roles. For this reason, they are responsible to the community, society, and the field of early childhood education for promoting the education and well-being of young children and their families.

Ideals

1-5.1 To provide the community with high-quality early care and education programs and services. (I-4.1)

I-5.2 To serve as a community resource, spokesperson, and advocate for quality programming for young children. To serve as a conduit between the community and programs by coordinating and collaborating with key community representatives.

I-5.3 To uphold the spirit as well as the specific provisions of applicable regulations and standards.

I-5.4 To increase the awareness of the public and policy makers about the importance of the early years and the positive impact of high-quality early care and education programs on society.

I-5.5 To advocate on behalf of children and families for high-quality programs and services for children and for professional development for the early childhood workforce.

I-5.6 To join with other early childhood educators in speaking with a clear and unified voice for the values of our profession on behalf of children, families, and early childhood educators.

I-5.7 To be an involved and supportive member of the early childhood profession.

I-5.8 To further the professional development of the field of early childhood education and to strengthen its commitment to realizing its core values as reflected in NAEYC's Code of Ethical Conduct and this Supplement. (I-4.8)

I-5.9 To ensure that adequate resources are provided so that all provisions of the Code of Ethical Conduct and this Supplement can be implemented.

Principles

P-5.1 We shall communicate openly and truthfully about the nature and extent of services that we provide. (P-4.1)

P-5.2 We shall apply for, accept, and work in positions for which we are personally well-suited and professionally qualified. We shall not offer services that we do not have the competence, qualifications, or resources to provide. (P-4.2)

P-5.3 We shall carefully check references and not hire or recommend for employment any person whose competence, qualifications, or character makes him or her unsuited for the position. (P-4.3)

P-5.4 When we make a personnel recommendation or serve as a reference, we shall be accurate and truthful.

P-5.5 We shall be objective and accurate in reporting the knowledge upon which we base our program practices. (P-4.4)

P-5.6 We shall be knowledgeable about the appropriate use of assessment strategies and instruments and interpret results accurately to families. (P-4.5)

P-5.7 We shall be familiar with laws and regulations that serve to protect the children in our programs and be vigilant in ensuring that these laws and regulations are followed. (P-4.6)

P-5.8 We shall hold program staff accountable for knowing and following all relevant standards and regulations.

P-5.9 When we become aware of a practice or situation that endangers the health, safety, or well-being of children, we have an ethical responsibility to protect children or inform parents and/or others who can. (P-4.7)

P-5.10 We shall not participate in practices in violation of laws and regulations that protect the children in our programs. (P-4.8)

P-5.11 When we have evidence that an early childhood program is violating laws or regulations protecting children, we shall report the violation to appropriate authorities who can be expected to remedy the situation. (P-4.9)

P-5.12 We shall be honest and forthright in communications with the public and with agencies responsible for regulation and accreditation.

P-5.13 When a program violates or requires its employees to violate NAEYC's Code of Ethical Conduct, it is permissible, after fair assessment of the evidence, to disclose the identity of that program. (P-4.10)

P-5.14 When asked to provide an informed opinion on issues, practices, products, or programs, we shall base our opinions on relevant experience, knowledge of child development, and standards of best practice.

Acknowledgments

This book is intended to help early childhood educators learn about ethics, the NAEYC Code of Ethical Conduct, and how they can apply the Code in their work with young children and families. The book rests on a strong foundation of ethical theory and NAEYC's more than 40 years of involvement with professional ethics.

We wish to express our deep appreciation to the following individuals who have contributed to our understanding of ethics and to this work.

Lilian Katz for her pioneering work on professional ethics in early childhood education and for consultation on the first edition of this book

Kenneth Kipnis for helping us learn about ethics and for his continuing interest and support

Marilyn Smith and **Barbara Bowman** for their belief early on that a code of ethics was important for early childhood educators

Peter Pizzolongo for championing NAEYC's work on professional ethics and for his contribution to the second edition

Robyn Chun, Eva Moravcik, Sherry Nolte, Christyn Dundorf, and **Ingrid Anderson** for their ongoing interest and encouragement

Ginger Fink and **Yasmin Grewal-Kök** for helping us think about issues related to young children's gender identity

Meir Muller for being a resource and sounding board on issues related to diversity and inclusiveness

Kathy Charner, editor-in-chief of Books and Related Resources at NAEYC, and **Holly Bohart,** senior editor at NAEYC, for their support, skilled guidance, and careful editing

Teachers, program administrators, adult educators, and others who have participated in classes and training sessions about ethics and discussions about cases in the Focus on Ethics column in *Young Children*. This book is the result of your work too

Our families—our husbands, Don Mickey and John Freeman, and Nancy's daughters, Gretchen and Nora, and their families for their interest, encouragement, and contributions to this book

About the Authors

Stephanie Feeney, PhD, is professor emerita of education at the University of Hawaii at Mānoa, where she taught undergraduate and graduate courses in early childhood education and directed the master's program in early childhood education.

Professor Feeney has written and lectured extensively on ethics and professionalism in early childhood education. She is the author of numerous articles and books, including *Professionalism in Early Childhood Education: Doing Our Best for Young Children*. She is coauthor of *Who Am I In the Lives of Children?,* now in its 11th edition, and *Continuing Issues in Early Childhood Education,* third edition.

Nancy K. Freeman, PhD, is professor emerita of education at the University of South Carolina in Columbia, where she was a member of the early childhood faculty. She taught graduate and undergraduate courses in early childhood education and did extensive work to support the professional development of the child care workforce, particularly those who work with infants and toddlers.

Professor Freeman has written and lectured extensively on professional ethics and has been involved in the Code's revisions and in the development of its supplements for program administrators and adult educators. She is also the lead author of *Planning and Administering Early Childhood Programs,* now in its 11th edition.

Both professors are coauthors of *Teaching the NAEYC Code of Ethical Conduct: A Resource Guide,* revised edition, and of the Focus on Ethics column that is a regular feature of NAEYC's journal, *Young Children.*

Discover NAEYC!

The National Association for the Education of Young Children (NAEYC) promotes high-quality early learning for all young children, birth through age 8, by connecting early childhood practice, policy, and research. We advance a diverse, dynamic early childhood profession and support all who care for, educate, and work on behalf of young children.

NAEYC members have access to award-winning publications, professional development, networking opportunities, professional liability insurance, and an array of members-only discounts.

Accreditation—NAEYC.org/accreditation

Across the country, **NAEYC Accreditation of Early Learning Programs** and **NAEYC Accreditation of Early Childhood Higher Education Programs** set the industry standards for quality in early childhood education. These systems use research-based standards to recognize excellence in the field of early childhood education.

Advocacy and Public Policy—NAEYC.org/policy

NAEYC is a leader in promoting and advocating for policies at the local, state, and federal levels that expand opportunities for all children to have equitable access to high-quality early learning. NAEYC is also dedicated to promoting policies that value early childhood educators and support their excellence.

Global Engagement—NAEYC.org/global

NAEYC's Global Engagement department works with governments and other large-scale systems to create guidelines to support early learning, as well as early childhood professionals throughout the world.

Professional Learning—NAEYC.org/ecp

NAEYC provides face-to-face training, technology-based learning, and Accreditation workshops—all leading to improvements in the knowledge, skills, and practices of early childhood professionals.

Publications and Resources—NAEYC.org/publications

NAEYC publishes some of the most valued resources for early childhood professionals, including award-winning books, *Teaching Young Children* magazine, and *Young Children*, the association's peer-reviewed journal. NAEYC publications focus on developmentally appropriate practice and enable members to stay up to date on current research and emerging trends, with information they can apply directly to their classroom practice.

Signature Events—NAEYC.org/events

NAEYC hosts three of the most important and well-attended annual events for educators, students, administrators, and advocates in the early learning community.

NAEYC's Annual Conference is the world's largest gathering of early childhood professionals.

NAEYC's Professional Learning Institute is the premier professional development conference for early childhood trainers, faculty members, researchers, systems administrators, and other professionals.

The **NAEYC Public Policy Forum** provides members with resources, training, and networking opportunities to build advocacy skills and relationships with policymakers on Capitol Hill.

Membership Options/Benefits

NAEYC.org/membership

NAEYC offers four membership categories*—Entry Level, Standard, Premium, and Family—each with a unique set of benefits.

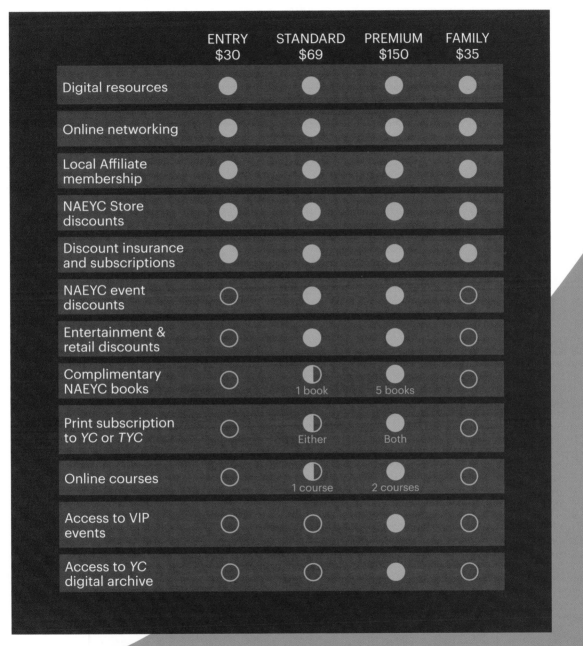

	ENTRY $30	STANDARD $69	PREMIUM $150	FAMILY $35
Digital resources	●	●	●	●
Online networking	●	●	●	●
Local Affiliate membership	●	●	●	●
NAEYC Store discounts	●	●	●	●
Discount insurance and subscriptions	●	●	●	●
NAEYC event discounts	○	●	●	○
Entertainment & retail discounts	○	●	●	○
Complimentary NAEYC books	○	◑ 1 book	● 5 books	○
Print subscription to *YC* or *TYC*	○	◑ Either	● Both	○
Online courses	○	◑ 1 course	● 2 courses	○
Access to VIP events	○	○	●	○
Access to *YC* digital archive	○	○	●	○

*Prices and benefits are subject to change. Check NAEYC.org for the most current information.